# Economic Ideas You Should Forget

Bruno S. Frey • David Iselin
Editors

# Economic Ideas You Should Forget

 Springer

*Editors*
Bruno S. Frey
University of Basel
CREMA
Zurich, Switzerland

David Iselin
KOF Swiss Economic Institute
ETH Zurich
Zurich, Switzerland

ISBN 978-3-319-47457-1     ISBN 978-3-319-47458-8   (eBook)
DOI 10.1007/978-3-319-47458-8

Library of Congress Control Number: 2017930404

Printed on acid-free paper

This Springer imprint is published by Springer Nature
The registered company is Springer International Publishing AG
The registered company address is: Gewerbestrasse 11, 6330 Cham, Switzerland

# Introduction

Ideas are the drivers behind innovation, may they be political, economic, in the arts or in science. "Nothing is as powerful as an idea whose time has come" is a popular quote attributed to Victor Hugo. But what about ideas whose time has already passed? Ideas that might have had value at a certain point in time but are still sticking around even though we should forget them?

In this book, we collect economic ideas whose time has passed and throw them into the dustbin of history. Economics has a sound base of theory supported by empirical research that is taught the same way all over the world. Yet, according to Popper, we gain scientific progress only by rejecting specific hypotheses within the theoretical framework. Economics is a vigorous and progressive science, which does not lose its force when particular parts of its theory are empirically rejected. Rather, they contribute to the accumulation of knowledge.

We bury ideas from the "Coase Theorem" to "Say's Law" to "Bayesianism". We let established scientists and lesser known younger colleagues speak. We give voice not only to economists but also to associates from other social sciences. We let economists from all fields speak and question ideas. We say goodbye to the positive effects of an abundance of choice; we bid farewell to the idea that economic growth increases people's well-being. We doubt that CEOs are paid so well merely because of their talent and question the usefulness of home ownership. Doubting assumptions and ideas is at the core of economics.

The essays do not idolize models or references and base their content on one single idea that should be forgotten. They reflect entirely personal views; the book therefore only contains contributions by single authors. This makes the content parsimonious and distinctive.

As editors, we deliberately allow for variety and did not interfere in any way with the authors' opinions. The diversity of ideas does not hinder but rather stimulates the discussion. It also does not come as a surprise that some economists would like to bury the same idea. The nuances in their respective argumentations are therefore especially attractive.

This book, although more a funeral than a birthday party, is not only about the past. Economics can be a joyful science. Burying old ideas lays the foundation for new ones. We are aware of the contradiction of writing down things that should be forgotten, yet the ideas we label "forgettable" are only preliminary and the label applies only under the existing institutional, social, and historical conditions. They may re-emerge under a different set of circumstances.

University of Basel                                          Bruno S. Frey
CREMA
Zurich, Switzerland

KOF Swiss Economic Institute                                David Iselin
ETH Zurich
Zurich, Switzerland

# Contents

**The End of Work**                                                         163
*Boris Zürcher*

**Postscript**                                                              165
*Bruno S. Frey and David Iselin*

# About the Editors

**Bruno S. Frey** is Permanent Visiting Professor at the University of Basel. He was Professor of Economics at the University of Zurich from 1977 to 2012; Distinguished Professor of Behavioural Science at the Business School of Warwick University, UK, from 2010 to 2013; and Senior Professor of Economics at Zeppelin University Friedrichshafen, Germany, from 2013 to 2015.

Frey is Research Director of CREMA—Centre for Research in Economics, Management and the Arts, Switzerland, and Co-Founder of CREW—Centre for Research in Economics and Well-being at the University of Basel. He was Managing Editor, from 1969 to 2015, and is now Honorary Editor of *Kyklos*. Bruno Frey seeks to extend economics beyond the standard neoclassics by including insights from other disciplines, including political science, psychology, and sociology.

**David Iselin** is an economist and member of the corporate communications team at KOF Swiss Economic Institute, ETH Zurich. He is editor of Ökonomenstimme, a policy platform for German-speaking economists. He holds a PhD of ETH Zurich. In his research he analyzes the relationship between news and the economy. As a freelance journalist, he is a regular contributor to the Swiss weekly DAS MAGAZIN, among others.

# Capitalism

Daron Acemoglu

>> *Capitalism has run its course, as we focus on the wrong things such as private ownership of capital. It's time to abandon the concept and concentrate on political and economic incentives forged by the broad complex of institutions.*

With roots extending back to Dutch, French, and English thinkers of the seventeenth and eighteenth centuries, the notion of capitalism has an impeccable intellectual pedigree and has been a mainstay of some of the most important philosophers of the nineteenth century, including Adam Smith, David Ricardo, Pierre-Joseph Proudhon, and Karl Marx. Despite this impressive historic cache, it is high time for academics to abandon it (and perhaps polemicists might one day follow). How could a notion that is so steeped in ideology be useful for academic discourse? For some, it is an economic system rooted in the crudest form of exploitation, always pregnant with injustice and inequality. For others, it is the unadulterated ideal of efficiency and dynamism, the best recipe for a fair society.

In fact, the definition of capitalism is full of contradictions. The most common is "an economic system based on private ownership of the means of production in their operation for profit." But other definitions make reference

D. Acemoglu (✉)
MIT, Cambridge, MA, USA

© Springer International Publishing AG 2017                                              **1**
B.S. Frey, D. Iselin (eds.), *Economic Ideas You Should Forget*,
DOI 10.1007/978-3-319-47458-8_1

to the "free market." For example, the *Oxford Dictionary of Economics* defines it as "an economic system in which private capital or wealth is used for the production and distribution of goods, and prices are determined mainly in a free market," while the *Merriam-Webster Dictionary* puts it as "an economic system characterized by private or corporate ownership of capital goods, by investments that are determined by private decision, and prices, production, and the distribution of goods that are determined mainly by competition in a free market." The "free market" is also a central tenet of Milton Friedman's definition of capitalism in *Capitalism and Freedom* and Ayn Rand's conception in *Capitalism: The Unknown Ideal.* The connotation, or perhaps even the exact equivalence, of the term free market with "perfectly competitive markets," notwithstanding other definitions, makes monopoly power and profits a defining aspect of capitalism (including in Marx's *Capital*, which christened "The General Law of Declining Profit" as a key characteristic of the capitalist system, and Sweezy and Baran's *Monopoly Capital*). But there isn't even agreement as to whether the presence of monopoly profits is a sin or a virtue. Though it is the former in many Marxist analyses, it is the driver of innovation and technological progress in Schumpeter's classic *Democracy, Capitalism, and Socialism.*

But most worrying is that emphasis on the ownership of the means of production, and particularly of capital, makes us focus on the wrong things. Is it useful to classify countries with reference to whether there is private ownership of capital? According to this demarcating line, both Egypt under Hosni Mubarak and social democratic Sweden are capitalist economies.

The root problem here is that for most of the problems we care about—how much shared prosperity, economic growth, technological progress, or social mobility a society will generate—whether there is (de jure) private ownership of capital is not much relevant. In *Why Nations Fail: The Origins of Power, Prosperity, and Poverty,* James Robinson and I have argued that many societies with different appearances have similar extractive economic institutions, which create a set of formal and informal rules to the advantage of politically powerful groups and at the expense of the rest of society. These extractive institutions also fail to generate incentives and opportunities for technological progress and sustained economic growth. In this respect, the extractive institutions of Mexico's "capitalist" economy have much more in common with North Korea's rigid communist system than with Swiss "capitalism."

Whether economic institutions are extractive, or at the other extreme inclusive, critically depends on political institutions. The notion of capitalism, by fixating on purely economic relations such as the ownership of capital and the means of production, misdirects our focus away from the *political economy*—and politics—of the economic arrangements a society has ended up with.

It's time to abandon this notion and concentrate on political and economic incentives forged by the broad complex of institutions.

# Sola Protestantism in Economics

## Rüdiger Bachmann

> **»** *Economists are at their best when they think in alternatives, with costs and benefits attached. So let's forget about "sola statements," a kind of protestant rigorism that still haunts parts of economics.*

Sola scriptura, sola fide, and sola gratia—these are the three sola principles that the Protestant reformers set against the Catholic church of their days. While I leave it to others to discuss the theology of this debate, I confess sympathy for the intellectual liberalism inherent in the Catholic resistance toward these sola principles. As an economist, I believe we have far too long adhered to our own sola principles, which has hurt the discipline. Protestant rigorism should be dead in economics.

To be clear, rejecting sola principles is not tantamount to accepting "anything goes." The statement "No critical social theory in economics" is not equivalent to a sola principle, because we cannot fully know the totality of what constitutes (good) economics. By contrast, rejecting sola principles in economics means keeping economics an open field. Catholic thought echoes such openness: for instance, the dogma of Christ's human and divine nature is a rejection of sola statements—Christ is (super)human; versus Christ is god, and his historical manifestation merely a simulation of human existence. What

R. Bachmann (✉)
University of Notre Dame, Notre Dame, IN, USA

© Springer International Publishing AG 2017                                    **5**
B.S. Frey, D. Iselin (eds.), *Economic Ideas You Should Forget*,
DOI 10.1007/978-3-319-47458-8_2

it really means to be human *and* divine is left as an unknowable mystery. Applied to economics, it is impossible to define (good) economics as sola principles try to do, but it is easy to recognize bad or, simply, non-economics (critical social theory). Below are three examples.

## Sola Actio

Economists have long insisted that the only relevant data are about actions: consumption, investment, hiring, firing, etc. Such data can be found in official national statistics, firm balance sheets, and, more recently, from household scanners. Other social sciences have been more liberal and used surveys to gather data on expectations, attitudes, subjective reasons, etc. Economists, by contrast, have often dismissed such data. For some, even unemployment data is meaningless, as the concept of job search cannot be adequately captured. Another example is expectations, paramount to economic theorizing, which have often been declared as outside the realm of objects against which economic theories can be tested. The rational expectation construct, where expectations are provided from inside an economic model, facilitated this dismissive attitude, which is slowly changing. And it should change. Albeit noisy, survey data contain valuable information. And here is a secret: national accounting data also require lots of assumptions and estimates—get the price of capital slightly wrong and capital stock estimates are way off.

## Sola Theoria

"It takes a model to beat a model," thus goes an old saying in economics. It is a sola statement and I think it is wrong. Data can beat a model, too. A business cycle model that produces countercyclical investment is, plainly, wrong, and so is one that makes consumption more volatile than GDP. There are basic facts that can beat models.

## Solus Grexitus

Many economists have argued that only a Grexit can save Greece, another sola statement and merely an example of a myriad of sola statements in policy advising. Politicians replied: a Grexit is off the table, what other options do we have? Economists: politicians are stupid; we are not accepting this constraint. Politicians: then you are useless to us. There are always alternatives. Economists are at their best when they explain these alternatives with costs and benefits attached, even when they think that a constraint is political and, in their views, unjustified and artificial.

Forget sola economics!

# Economics Has Nothing to Do with Religion

Sascha O. Becker

**»** *Economists usually don't bother too much about religion. That's a mistake. Protestant areas of Prussia had higher literacy rates than Catholic areas. And higher education went hand in hand with better economic development.*

A popular view is that economics is about inflation, unemployment, prices, and quantities, but not about religion or culture. And surely, soft factors such as religion do not matter for economic outcomes? Not surprisingly, students of economics would not typically come across these in their lectures on microeconomics, macroeconomics, or econometrics. When economic issues are debated in the media, they do not feature highly, but religion matters for economics and economics matters for religion.

Max Weber famously discussed a link between Protestantism and the spirit of capitalism, but he is often viewed as a founder of sociology and not as an economist. In fact, he was probably both: he held the Chair of National Economics in Munich, and he contributed to a variety of disciplines in the social sciences. Weber's view that religion matters for economic development was often dismissed, but his claim that Protestants are better off than Catholics has been confirmed in various recent studies. For instance, Protestant areas of

S.O. Becker (✉)
University of Warwick, Coventry, UK

© Springer International Publishing AG 2017
B.S. Frey, D. Iselin (eds.), *Economic Ideas You Should Forget,*
DOI 10.1007/978-3-319-47458-8_3

**9**

nineteenth-century Prussia, where Weber was born and where the Protestant Reformation started in 1517, were economically more advanced than Catholic areas. What explains this difference? The Protestant Reformation was not just about religious beliefs and differences in liturgy. Martin Luther's wish for every believer to be able to read the Bible was a daunting task at a time when only a tiny minority of his sixteenth-century contemporaries were able to read and write. The Protestant reformers set out to change that. Luther urged rulers across the Protestant lands to build and maintain schools, and he urged parents to send their children to school. His efforts were supported by various other reformers, foremost by Philipp Melanchthon, the "Praeceptor Germaniae," the educator of Germany. And in fact, in nineteenth-century Prussia, Protestant areas had more schools per square kilometer and higher literacy rates. Higher education went hand in hand with better economic development. Weber was right that religion matters for economic development, but probably not because of his purported Protestant ethic, but simply because Protestants put more emphasis on education.

Not only did Protestant regions benefit by getting more education earlier than Catholic regions. Protestant regions also displayed a lower gender gap in education. Again, the root of this development can be traced back to the Reformation itself. Luther urged Protestant rulers not only to maintain schools, but he explicitly mentions girls' schools. Historic evidence shows that, in Protestant areas, not only boys' schools but also girls' schools were built. As a result, in nineteenth-century Prussia, the gap in literacy rates between men and women was smaller in Protestant areas than in Catholic areas, documenting the success of these early emancipatory efforts.

There are two sides of the same coin: while Protestantism can be seen to have had positive effects on economic development, an alternative reading is that Catholicism has held it back.

The reverse is also true: religious organizations follow economic incentives. Churches may behave like firms. It has been argued that, before the Reformation, the Catholic church behaved like a monopolist. Modern Pentecostal churches have been studied as multinational firms. What is clear is that religion does matter when it comes to economics.

# More Choice Is Always Better

Christine Benesch

>> *More choice seems in any case to be superior to less choice. However, that does not hold true in all situations. The abundance of choice can have huge transaction and psychological costs.*

When walking through the aisles of a supermarket, we can choose between dozens of breakfast cereals and potato chips. Amazon offers several hundred varieties of dishwashing liquid and laundry detergent. As we step into our favorite coffee shop, we can have our coffee as a blonde, medium, or dark roast; brewed with beans from Guatemala, Vietnam, or Tanzania; with or without milk, skimmed, soy, or rice milk; with caramel, chocolate, or hazelnut flavor; hot or cold; large or small. On Netflix or iTunes, we can watch not only the latest movies and TV shows but also all the classics and evergreens. The abundant choice offers a satisfying option to everyone—no matter how special his or her tastes. In addition, competition between brands and suppliers drives prices down and quality up. It is therefore no surprise that economists generally view more choice as beneficial.

The abundance of choice is, however, associated with costs that might outweigh the benefits and are usually disregarded in economic theory. Choosing can entail huge transaction costs. Evaluating all the potential options takes

C. Benesch (✉)
University of St. Gallen, St. Gallen, Switzerland

© Springer International Publishing AG 2017                     **11**
B.S. Frey, D. Iselin (eds.), *Economic Ideas You Should Forget*,
DOI 10.1007/978-3-319-47458-8_4

up valuable time, which people could spend on more enjoyable activities. Beyond these pure opportunity costs of time, choice can have psychological costs as well. People are afraid to make wrong decisions, and, because of loss aversion and hindsight bias, they may regret missed opportunities and suffer even more if their choices turn out badly. In the famous jam experiment by Sheena Iyengar from Columbia University and Mark Lepper from Stanford University, customers in a supermarket could sample jams from a set of either 6 or 24 varieties and received a one-dollar discount if they subsequently bought a jam. Those customers exposed to the larger set were ten times less likely to actually buy a jam. In order to avoid complex decisions with too many options, people prefer not to choose at all. And even if they do choose, they are less satisfied with their choice and feel more regret.

Even those who find it less difficult to make up their mind might make choices that clash with their long-term interest. When having to trade off short-term gains versus long-term costs, many people exhibit self-control problems or weakness of will. The availability of many enjoyable options to choose from can exacerbate this problem. My own research (together with Bruno S. Frey and Alois Stutzer) shows that, in countries with a high average choice of TV channels, those people who spend many hours watching TV report lower levels of life satisfaction. A potential explanation of this finding is that such viewers have self-control problems with regard to their TV consumption. When facing the trade-off between the immediate gratification of TV consumption and its long-term costs, for example, lack of sleep, these individuals watch more TV than planned or considered optimal ex ante and ex post. As a consequence, they regret their choice. In short, when having many suitable TV programs at their disposal, viewers find it more difficult to resist temptation. TV-on-demand offers such as Netflix, where one's favorite movies and TV shows are available around the clock, may aggravate the problem.

The jam and TV examples illustrate that more choice is not always better. Hence, economists should not disregard the trade-off between the benefits and costs of a larger choice set.

# People Are Outcome Oriented

## Matthias Benz

**»** *It's usually assumed that people derive satisfaction from outcomes, like higher salaries. But then it's difficult to explain why the self-employed are happier with their work than employees, although their income is lower. The reason lies in the process of how the self-employed earn their money.*

Economics is very much based on the idea that people care about outcomes. If they work, they work for money. If they judge politics, they think about the benefits of public policies. If they look at inequality—to name a very current topic—they worry about the unequal distribution of income and wealth.

But there is more to human welfare than outcomes. The process also matters. People attach value to the process through which outcomes like money, public policies, or inequality are achieved. While outcomes clearly are relevant, economics needs to integrate the process to account for human utility and behavior.

Looking at self-employed people, a large literature shows that, on average, they earn less than employees in firms. A typical economist would tend to think they are worse off and are making a mistake in pursuing self-employment. But a new literature shows that, perhaps surprisingly, the self-

M. Benz (✉)
Neue Zürcher Zeitung, Zurich, Switzerland

© Springer International Publishing AG 2017
B.S. Frey, D. Iselin (eds.), *Economic Ideas You Should Forget*,
DOI 10.1007/978-3-319-47458-8_5

employed derive greater satisfaction from their work than the employed. So, in terms of overall utility, they are in fact better off. This higher satisfaction derives from the process of how they earn their living. Self-employed workers are their own boss, while employed workers have to take orders from superiors. This reflects the difference between the two most important decision-making procedures in economic life: markets and hierarchies. People seem to attach a value to the freedom they enjoy on markets, in contrast to the lack of freedom in hierarchies.

Looking at decision-making in politics, democracy is typically seen as superior because it leads to better public policies and higher welfare. But democracy is also a procedure and delegates decisions to citizens. A new literature shows that citizens value the right to decide irrespective of the outcome. Thus, democracy is a source of utility, beyond gross domestic product and other measures of economic outcomes. This holds particularly for more direct forms of democracy like in Switzerland.

Looking at inequality, the rising inequality of income and wealth in very advanced countries like the USA is currently widely discussed. However, while inequality may be high in the USA, it is also high in less advanced countries such as the Ukraine. But people would judge these instances of inequality quite differently. Inequality is despised by Ukrainians, because it is a result of an unfair oligarchic system. Americans find inequality more acceptable, because in principle everybody has the chance to "make it." Similarly, most people don't object to the wealth accumulated by successful entrepreneurs or sports stars, which is seen as fair and "deserved." Interestingly, the current debate on inequality started after top managers were starting to amass large fortunes, which is suspected to have happened in unfair ways.

Process should be taken seriously in economics and economic policy. If you get the process right, you increase human well-being.

# Deriving People's Trade Policy Preferences from Macroeconomic Trade Theory

Thomas Bernauer

» *Public opinion concerning international trade is shaped mostly by noneconomic factors and heuristic cues. Trying to explain support for trade by purely economic reasoning is therefore doomed to fail.*

In democratic societies, policy-makers supply protectionist trade policies as a result of interest group pressure and demand by the public. However, explaining variation in protectionist demand across groups and individuals is far from trivial. Why most farmers want trade protection, and often obtain it, is easy to explain from a political economy viewpoint. Their per capita benefits from trade protection are usually high, and the low per capita costs of protection are spread across all consumers and taxpayers. But it is far less obvious why the public, to which policy-makers also pay a lot of attention, often supports protectionist policies, too. Related to that, one may wonder why international trade liberalization efforts focus so much on reciprocal steps, though orthodox trade economics tells us that even unilateral market opening is beneficial.

The reason is that, at least in theory, free trade benefits countries as a whole, but benefits some individuals within a given society and hurts others. This

T. Bernauer (✉)
ETH Zurich, Zurich, Switzerland

© Springer International Publishing AG 2017
B.S. Frey, D. Iselin (eds.), *Economic Ideas You Should Forget*,
DOI 10.1007/978-3-319-47458-8_6

**15**

provides the main entry point for economic theorizing about individual preferences and public opinion on trade issues. Since macroeconomic models of trade are ultimately based on the *homo economicus* assumption, we can derive expectations about individuals' trade preferences from these models. Arguably, the key hypothesis derived from trade models is that free trade benefits those people in a country who own abundant factors of production and disadvantages owners of scarce factors and that it favors investors and workers in export-oriented industries with a comparative advantage. This means that, in highly industrialized countries, skilled labor and capital owners as well as those working and/or investing in competitive export-oriented industries are likely to support free trade.

Alas, the empirical evidence for these claims is weak. Trade policy preferences seem to be influenced more by general worldviews, political ideology, environmental attitudes, social trust, and other noneconomic factors, rather than economic self-interest. In addition, even when people form their trade preferences partly based on economic considerations, those considerations tend to be sociotropic rather than egotropic (i.e., people think more about what is good for their country than what is good for themselves).

Perhaps the main reason why people seem to resort to general beliefs, attitudes, or worldviews, rather than economic utility, in forming their trade preferences is limited information. Most people know very little about trade economics nor are they willing to invest time and effort to acquire such knowledge. Many if not most individuals may thus simply not be able or willing to figure out how trade liberalization has affected or will affect them economically.

However, think for a moment about the implications of educating the public in trade economics. Would that make people more comfortable with free trade? A recent survey experiment by Rho and Tomz explores this. They find that more knowledge about economic efficiency and welfare effects of free trade tend to make people more supportive of free trade. But "treating" people with information on who in society is likely to win or lose from trade liberalization (distributional cues) tends to polarize society more. It seems to induce more self-serving trade preferences among more educated people and more other-serving trade preferences among less educated people. My (simplistic) take on these findings is that it is not at all obvious that educating the population in trade economics would eventually result in greater public support for free trade.

In brief, public opinion concerning international trade is shaped mostly by noneconomic factors and heuristic cues. Deriving predictions of individual preferences from the most cherished macroeconomic trade models is, both in analytical and policy-related terms, not very useful.

# Size (of Government) Doesn't Matter

Tim Besley

**»** *Advocating for a small government share for its own sake is misleading. Effective and large governments have common roots. More important than size are constraints on the government.*

For a market economy to flourish, government needs to be constrained, but it need not be small. Among the richest economies in the world are the Nordics (Denmark, Norway, and Sweden) which seem to thrive (over a wide range of metrics) in spite of their high taxes and public spending. The twentieth century saw the government share in GDP rise from around 10 % to 40 % along with rising living standards. Countries with large governments tend also to have effective governments. The focus should be on why this does not happen everywhere.

The Nordic countries are an example of a development cluster where peace, high income, and effective government coincide. This is confirmed by four measures of state effectiveness: (1) they have high scores in upholding the rule of law according to the World Justice Project, (2) they respect personal freedoms according to Freedom House, (3) they have low corruption according to Transparency International, and (4) they are market-friendly according to the World Bank Doing Business ranking.

T. Besley (✉)
London School of Economics, London, UK

© Springer International Publishing AG 2017                                **17**
B.S. Frey, D. Iselin (eds.), *Economic Ideas You Should Forget*,
DOI 10.1007/978-3-319-47458-8_7

At the other extreme are countries which perform badly on a whole range of indicators. However, there is an Anna Karenina principle. While all functioning countries seem alike, poorly functioning countries are unhappy (and non-functioning) in idiosyncratic ways. Yet, rarely is the problem one of taxing too much. Poor countries around the world tend to have a tax take in GDP which is similar to today's affluent countries a century ago (10 % – 20 %).

An effective government and large government have common roots. When governments deliver, their citizens are willing to entrust them with more of their money and to intervene more widely.

But what factors promote an effective government? Government works best when its actions are limited by constraints of two main forms: (1) constraints on executive power which come from an independent judiciary, active media, and legislative oversight to scrutinize government actions and enforce rules and (2) poorly performing policy-makers must be removed which is facilitated by open elections, a well-educated citizenry, and a strong civil society. Creating effective institutions requires supporting democratic values; governments who try to weaken constraints must know that their citizens will protest.

All governments engage in redistribution. When government is constrained, such redistribution takes place in a transparent and rule-driven way, and it is more likely that spending upholds common interests. A good example is mass health-care funding and social security which redistribute resources over the life cycle to the benefit of most citizens. Funding these programs with broad-based, progressive taxation, such as a VAT or income tax, rather than using selective and arbitrary forms of revenue generation, has become an accepted principle of constrained government.

Without strong constraints, governments redistribute resources to support narrow interests in economically damaging ways. They might grant monopolies to political cronies, expropriate the successful, and use protection and regulations to create rents for the ruling elite. These have adverse consequences for innovation and growth.

Once government spends a large slice of the pie (around 40 % in many advanced countries), it has a stake in maintaining an effective private sector to fund the state. This explains why protecting property rights and low corruption are priorities in large states. The benefits from broad tax bases and common-interest spending and regulation dwarf deadweight losses from high taxes.

Those who decry a large government often fail to appreciate the difference between a constrained government and a small government. They are right to criticize interventionists who do not appreciate the role of a supporting institutional framework. But advocating a small government share for its own sake is dystopian and no guarantee of freedom. When it comes to the promotion of prosperity along with economic, social, and political freedoms, it is the large and effective states built on appropriately designed constraints on government that are leading the way.

# Bayesianism

## Ken Binmore

---

**»** *Bayesianism has a role in microeconomics and game theory, but is utterly misplaced in macroeconomics and finance.*

---

Bayesian decision theory was invented by Leonard (Jimmy) Savage in his *Foundations of Statistics* of 1954. Bayesianism is the doctrine that his theory always applies to everything. In particular, Savage's subjective probabilities (reflecting the odds at which someone would be indifferent to betting a small amount for or against an event) are mindlessly taken to be epistemic probabilities (reflecting the logical degree of belief to be attached to an event given the available evidence).

Savage emphatically rejects the latter interpretation. He recalls two proverbs: "Look before you leap" and "Cross that bridge when you come to it." He then confines his theory to situations in which the first of these proverbs has been exhaustively applied under all possible contingencies. He acknowledges that meeting this requirement is impossible in large or complex worlds and so urges us to apply his theory only in small worlds. On page 16 of his book, he says that it would be "utterly ridiculous" and "preposterous" to use his theory elsewhere.

K. Binmore (✉)
University College London, London, UK

© Springer International Publishing AG 2017
B.S. Frey, D. Iselin (eds.), *Economic Ideas You Should Forget*,
DOI 10.1007/978-3-319-47458-8_8

Savage's famous encounter with Maurice Allais in Paris illustrates how he thought Bayesian decision theory should be used in practice. When it was pointed out that his answers to what is now called the Allais paradox were inconsistent, he revised them until they were consistent. Luce and Raiffa's *Games and Decisions* summarizes his views as follows:

"Once confronted with inconsistencies, one should, so the argument goes, modify one's initial decisions so as to be consistent. Let us assume that this jockeying—making snap judgments, checking up on their consistency, modifying them, again checking on consistency etc.—leads ultimately to a bona fide, prior distribution."

Savage's rational agents therefore do not begin with a prior from which they deduce their posteriors. They begin by guessing at posteriors and then massage their guesses until consistency has been achieved. The prior is then derived from the system of massaged posteriors. Rational agents are therefore not somehow endowed with a prior. They have to work hard at constructing a prior. They certainly do not choose whatever prior reflects an initial state of complete ignorance. Such a methodology is as far from Savage's view on constructing priors as it is possible to be. Instead of using all potentially available information in the small world to be studied in formulating a prior, it treats all such information as irrelevant.

If this story is taken seriously, we are in desperate need of some Schumpeterian creative destruction. Microeconomics and game theory are safe and so are versions of Bayesian statistics that are defended against classical statistics purely on empirical grounds. But the worlds of macroeconomics and finance are not just large, but hopelessly and irredeemably large. So I say, throw out all applications of Bayesian decision theory in macroeconomics and finance—though the sky fall. Whatever new theory emerges from the flames might even work.

# The Return on Equity

## Urs Birchler

**»** *The fixation on the return on equity (RoE) in banking is dangerous. It is both conceptually and strategically flawed. RoE targets should be abandoned right away.*

The banking industry still uses the return on equity (RoE) as a measure of performance and as an instrument of internal capital allocation. Some bankers even claim they have to aim at high RoE targets in order to cover the return on capital (RoC) required by shareholders.

This may sound plausible at first sight. However, as many authors have laid out, the fixation on the RoE has no logical basis. It has even been identified as one of the factors behind the financial crisis of 2007–2008.

The return on capital required to satisfy shareholders is:

$$RoC = Riskfree\ Rate + Risk\ Premium.$$

A conceptually sound performance measure is a company's annual return on assets (RoA):

U. Birchler (✉)
University of Zurich, Zurich, Switzerland

© Springer International Publishing AG 2017                                    **23**
B.S. Frey, D. Iselin (eds.), *Economic Ideas You Should Forget*,
DOI 10.1007/978-3-319-47458-8_9

$$\text{RoA} = \text{Return}/\text{Assets} = \text{Riskfree Rate} + \text{Risk Premium} + \text{Ability},$$

RoA minus RoC measures ability ex post. Unfortunately, the RoA is not immune against manipulation if managers can take up unobservable risk.

Yet, the RoE is worse. It is defined as:

$$\text{RoE} = \text{Return}/\text{Equity} = (\text{Return}/\text{Assets}) \times (\text{Assets}/\text{Equity})$$
$$= \text{RoA} \times \text{Leverage}$$

The RoE thus can be increased not only by (potentially unobservable) asset risk but also by higher leverage. Unfortunately, both asset risk and leverage can bankrupt a company.

This is true for any company, but the RoE is particularly disastrous in banking. First, in financial affairs, unobservable risks abound. Second, banking is one of the most leveraged industries; even a small change in the capital level therefore has a strong impact on the RoE. Third, many banks are "systemically important," i.e., their risks are partly borne by taxpayers.

Notwithstanding these problems, the RoE it is still widely used. In a recent study on the financial crisis (August 2013), Christophe Moussu finds that, even after the crisis, managerial compensation is highly related to the RoE (but not to the RoA), even though "the pre-crisis RoE has a strong impact on the destruction of value for shareholders."

This leaves but one conclusion: The RoE as a performance measure—at least in banking—is not only conceptually flawed. Worse, the flaws are used strategically by managers. Bank managers' compensation is tied directly or indirectly to the RoE, giving them incentive to (ab)use their power to manipulate RoE figures by burdening their banks with unobservable risk and by pushing leverage up to the legal maximum.

Bank CEOs sometimes defend their double-digit RoE targets, blaming their investors for demanding such enormous yields, "What else could they do!" While a bank is not viable in the long run if it fails to produce returns sufficient to cover their cost of funding, these CEOs are putting the cart before the horse. The required return on capital (RoC) is not a fixed figure. It increases with a firm's risk premium and leverage—along the same lines as the RoA and RoE defined above. A CEO trying to lift the RoE but not the RoC (by means other than ability) would need to be a second Baron Munchausen who pulled himself and the horse he was riding on out of a mire by his own hair.

Analysts themselves occasionally fall into the RoE trap. While investors, particularly those big enough to have a direct line to the CEO, should be expected to understand the flaws of the RoE, they may not bother as long as banks are too-big-to-fail and the risks will ultimately be borne by the taxpayer. Bank CEOs pretend not to understand the devastating impact of RoE targets, and why should they: In today's economy, this inability is one of the best-paid abilities.

# Peak Oil Theory

## Charles B. Blankart

**»** *"Peak oil" theory is driven by thinking in dependencies, not in exchange: It predicts crises which do not occur and misses to handle crises which occur. Time to let it go.*

Most economic theories are wrong. Fortunately, most wrong theories are irrelevant. But some wrong theories are relevant. One of these latter theories is Marion King Hubbert's peak oil theory, postulated in 1956. Hubbert was a geologist who thought that oil exploration is an uncertain undertaking. Frequently, drilling is *en vain*; in a few cases, gas is discovered and in another few cases oil. Given uncertainty, only proven reserves are said to be reliable. Proven reserves appear as a peak in the known graphs. In lucky times, we find ourselves on the ascending part of the bell-shaped curve. In less favorable times, we slip downward on the descending part of Hubbert's peak. Oil reserves dwindle and might come to an end. Hubbert's peak oil theory is still popular, but doubly false: It predicts crises which do not occur and misses to handle crises which occur.

On the one hand, scientists have regularly made projections in application of Hubbert's peak oil theory which never materialized. In 2008, the renowned geologist and Stanford professor Gilbert Masters concluded that: "It's About

C.B. Blankart (✉)
Humboldt-University, Berlin, Germany

© Springer International Publishing AG 2017                          **27**
B.S. Frey, D. Iselin (eds.), *Economic Ideas You Should Forget*,
DOI 10.1007/978-3-319-47458-8_10

Forty Years Until the Oil Runs Out." In 2004, Claudia Kemfert, the chief energy economist of the German Institute of Economic Research, reported that the global oil reserves would last only for another 15 years [up to 2019]. Should she be wrong and oil will still be available in 2019, peak oil theorists will say to Little Red Riding Hood: "Be aware, not this time, but the next time the wolf will most certainly come."

On the other hand, peak oil theory, as other theories, could not predict the OPEC oil embargo of 1973, but more importantly, it was unable to offer a solution on how to approach such an unexpected event. In his desperate search for a workable solution, President Nixon took action and imposed rationing by gasoline price ceilings in 1973–1974 which made an outgrown crisis out of the initial cutoff.

The lesson from the OPEC crisis is that crises occur where free market forces are restricted by state intervention. Different from the US government, the European governments reacted to the OPEC cutoff with laissez-faire. Prices rose for a while, but queues did not appear. The US government wanted to be smarter than the markets, but failed. Practice shows that oil companies apply a simple theory. In the short run, they maneuver their tankers toward places of scarcity, and they increase exploitation of existing oil wells. In the middle and long run, they intensify discovery at higher marginal costs as reserves are a function of oil price and technology. Therefore, Hubbert's peak is shifting continuously to the right. It appears as a red line of successive peaks, not as a single peak. Apparently, the reserves to production ratio has increased only slowly reflecting oil companies' expectations.

Were the US government to think in terms of costs of reserves, oil supply could be maintained at little marginal cost. But political scientists seem to have won the battle in consulting the US administration. They typically think in dependence and not in exchange. If Arab potentates are brought in dependence of US arms, then they might also maintain oil supply. Such an interpretation might explain the extraordinary arms delivery contracts of 1.3 billion USD between the USA and Saudi Arabia in 2015. For Little Red Riding Hood is taught: "Be sure, next time the wolf will come."

# More Choice Is Always Better

## Alan S. Blinder

> **»** *Standard economic theory told us: If you have more choices, your utility must either rise or be unchanged. Don't be fooled. Sometimes less choice is better.*

Here's something that we all know to be wrong in our everyday lives, but which our economist union card bans us from believing while we're on the job: *Utility is nondecreasing in the number of choices.*

We all learned this principle as one of the fundamental axioms of choice early in our economic educations. If your choice set is augmented by the addition of more choices, your utility must either rise or be unchanged. It cannot go down.

But it's false! All *homo sapiens* know that more choices can confuse or even overwhelm you. To weigh all the alternatives takes time (a scarce resource), may be a source of anxiety, and may even impose explicit costs on the decisionmaker. We humans are liable, maybe even likely, to make mistakes and choose the wrong option. We certainly think so—and that's aggravating. When two options are pretty close to being on the same indifference curve, it can be painful (and time-consuming) to decide which we prefer. Even though

A.S. Blinder (✉)
Princeton University, Princeton, NJ, USA

© Springer International Publishing AG 2017                    **29**
B.S. Frey, D. Iselin (eds.), *Economic Ideas You Should Forget*,
DOI 10.1007/978-3-319-47458-8_11

*homo economicus* assures us the choice doesn't matter much, we don't believe him.

In a famous marketing experiment in a grocery store, more jam was sold when the display table offered six free samples than when it offered 24. There are other such examples. I find myself in such situations regularly. Couldn't I just have two or three options?

The fallacy of more choices is not just an amusing curiosity.

At the level of pure theory, it undermines standard utility theory and, by dint of that, most of welfare economics. If utility can *decrease* in the number of choices, the edifice of welfare economics at least teeters and probably crumbles—and the virtue of the Invisible Hand goes with it.

At the level of policy, the fallacy highlights the role of good default options. A benevolent (what an important adjective!) government that circumscribes your choices can actually make you better off, not in theory, but in practice.

# (Un)Productive Labor

## Monika Bütler

**»** *The focus on labor productivity in analyzing a country's performance is misleading. It is even not good at assessing productivity itself. Let us ignore the concept and tackle the real problems in economic performance head on.*

Every now and then, the OECD comes up with a devastating verdict for rich countries. Most recently: mediocre labor productivity.

Labor productivity is suggestive of an easily measurable concept and a suitable policy instrument. Unfortunately, neither is true. Labor productivity is simply a leftover measure after decomposing GDP into yearly hours worked, employment share, and participation rate.

While labor productivity is not the most intelligent measure to target in the first place, it is also not a meaningful concept to assess the effectiveness of a country's labor force.

To illustrate why, let us compare two hypothetical countries. Both of their populations have the same training and inherent productivity, the same level of technology, and the same capital stock per head. There are at least three reasons why the measured labor productivity of these otherwise identical countries may diverge.

M. Bütler (✉)
University of St. Gallen, St. Gallen, Switzerland

© Springer International Publishing AG 2017
B.S. Frey, D. Iselin (eds.), *Economic Ideas You Should Forget*,
DOI 10.1007/978-3-319-47458-8_12

First, the integration of less productive individuals in the labor market: A country that keeps its less productive citizens employed (rather than shuttling them into transfer programs) automatically has a lower labor productivity. If the USA had an employed labor force of only Mark Zuckerberg and Bill Gates, its labor productivity would be extremely high. Would the USA be better off? No, because even though Zuckerberg and Gates are immensely productive, their income is far too low to feed the US population. However, even normal workers benefit from wider integration of less productive individuals: Their disposable income is higher because fewer taxes are required to finance transfers.

Second, different working hours: If workers are more productive in the first few hours of a workday than at the end, then the country with a longer work week automatically ends up with lower labor productivity. Which of the two countries' citizens are better off is debatable: In economic terms, there is a trade-off between disposable income (higher in the "less productive" country) and leisure (higher in the country with the higher labor productivity); however, consumption income and per capita GDP are certainly higher in the "less productive" country.

Third, labor market participation of highly skilled workers, in particular among the elderly and women: The fewer hours well-educated individuals work, the lower is the measured labor productivity. This is, of course, a problem if highly skilled women and elderly workers stay out of the labor force, not by choice, but because high marginal tax rates, social security system's disincentives, or missing child-care facilities prevent them from working.

Is low labor productivity then a symptom of an underlying problem in economic policy? Perhaps, but the optimal policy response crucially depends on the cause of this low labor productivity.

A much better strategy is to ignore labor productivity and tackle the real problems in economic performance head on. If there are sheltered sectors in the economy, liberalize them. If the highly skilled retire too early, give them incentives to stay on. If mothers leave the labor market, improve child care and school facilities and reduce the tax on the second earner.

Last but not least, research has shown that the feeling of "being needed" is as important for vulnerable groups of the population as material security. A lower labor productivity, thus, is the price to pay for better social integration.

# Volatility Is Risk

## Peter Cauwels

>> *Volatility in financial markets is seen as risk. That is misleading. Volatility is usually the lowest at the crest of a bubble and the highest at the trough of a crash, contrary to risk that moves exactly in the other direction.*

According to the efficient market hypothesis, asset prices always trade at their fair value, which is the result of the aggregation of all available information in the market system. This fair value is spiced up with a significant noise component (quantified by volatility), associated with economic variability and endogenous trading. The more noisy, or volatile, an asset is, the higher any deviation of the actual market price from the fair value can be. By construction, the observation of a stronger volatility is interpreted as a higher risk. As a result of these assumptions, the dynamics of financial markets become extremely simple: the most probable price of tomorrow is the price of today, augmented by taking into consideration the risk resulting from volatility. This leads to an anticipated excess return (or relative change of prices above the risk-free rate), which should be proportional to the volatility.

P. Cauwels (✉)
Department of Management Technology and Economics, ETH Zurich, Zürich, Switzerland

© Springer International Publishing AG 2017      **33**
B.S. Frey, D. Iselin (eds.), *Economic Ideas You Should Forget*,
DOI 10.1007/978-3-319-47458-8_13

This idea that volatility is risk (and should be remunerated) should be forgotten.

Financial markets are not at equilibrium. Rather, the norm is that they are continuously punctuated by regimes of exuberance (bubbles) ending in crashes or strong corrections. Typically, investors are often enticed into buying an asset, attracted by the prospect of extrapolated higher returns and moved by the social forces of imitation. When investors buy because the price goes up and/or others do the same, a feedback mechanism sets off that fuels a spiraling growth away from equilibrium. This bubble is mirrored by the crash that follows, fueled by the selling of traders reacting to previous decreases, pushing the price further down in a spiraling crash. Both bubbles and crashes are the result of imitation and herd behavior, which push the market price far away from equilibrium, beyond the mere effect of noise. Such processes are unsustainable and finally result in a systemic failure. This constitutes the real risk in financial markets.

Moreover, many studies have shown that an asset's volatility is negatively correlated with its return. This "leverage effect" refers to the fact that, when asset prices drop, volatility increases and vice versa. In the past years, this anomaly of low-risk stocks having higher expected returns has been exploited by portfolio managers using a strategy called "betting against beta."

Consider the situation in which investors are attracted into a market because of the prospect of higher returns. This sets off a feedback mechanism causing the price to spiral ever higher. During this development, as a consequence of the leverage effect, the volatility decreases. At some point, some investors start realizing that the process is no longer sustainable and the market collapses. The crash occurs because the market has entered an unstable phase. Like a ruler held up vertically on your finger, any small disturbance could have triggered the fall. Now, people start selling because the price goes down. A crash occurs and volatility shoots up. In hindsight, the volatility has been the lowest at the crest of the bubble, when the risk was the highest, right before the crash. In contrast, volatility is the highest at the trough of the crash, when the risk is the lowest, and a very interesting buying opportunity occurs for contrarians that know how to exploit the madness of crowds.

Volatility is risk? Clearly this is an economic idea that should be forgotten. No, volatility is opportunity!

# Robots Will Take All Our Jobs

Reto Cueni

> **»** *That the new machine age will lead to massive and persistent unemployment is the new soon-to-arrive doomsday scenario. But it's wrong. We should not underestimate the human capacity to react to external changes.*

The onset of a new technology and its implementation is almost always perceived as a threat to employment. What was true in the first industrial revolution is true again in the "second machine age" with its unprecedented development in information technology. We are afraid that this technology will not only replace humans as physical manpower or for simple repetitive tasks but give rise to machines that will start to substitute for human mental power and be able to learn by themselves.

I think we should move beyond the fear that the second machine age will lead to massive and persistent unemployment. Changes in employment due to new technology are inherently a question of complementarity and substitution. Naturally, a new technology usually substitutes for certain human tasks. Some jobs become redundant and are cut. Some people will become

---

The opinions expressed are those of the author and do not necessarily reflect the views of Vontobel Asset Management.

R. Cueni (✉)
Vontobel Asset Management, Zurich, Switzerland

© Springer International Publishing AG 2017                                    **35**
B.S. Frey, D. Iselin (eds.), *Economic Ideas You Should Forget*,
DOI 10.1007/978-3-319-47458-8_14

unemployed, and the fear of persistent unemployment arises. Yet, we tend to forget three points. First, the human brain and its needs and preferences are adaptive. Who would have thought, when a steam engine first powered an elevator, that some 150 years later, it is the norm that any house with more than two stories not only has an elevator, but also a light, sensors telling the automatic door when not to close, and an artificial voice to tell passengers on what floor they are. Today, we need these gadgets and, in fact, seek out even more fancy ones. Even only 50 years ago, an elevator only had to bring you to another floor.

Second, humans always worry about their relative, not their absolute, standing. The quest for a faster way home will not end even when new technology guides us home, bypassing all traffic jams. Everyone would like to be home a bit sooner or at least a bit sooner than their neighbors—so the quest continues.

Furthermore, there is the fear that this next machine age will be altogether different because of the unprecedented economies of scale of the digital revolution. With a simple mouse click, we can produce not only a copy of a particular song but several million copies. This could mean that the new technology will lead to a "superstar economy," where superstars earn an even bigger share of the pie, leading to ever greater inequality. In the new machine age, a few superstars can sell their products to everyone on the planet (or at least to the three quarters of the global population, according to the World Bank, that now have access to a mobile phone). Hence, ever fewer people will find a job in accordance with this thinking.

We are forgetting that humans will react to the new machines this time as they have all previous times. Imagine you are a very specialized artist creating art that only one person in a million would pay for. Twenty years ago, you had no chance to make a living. These days, you might reach this one-millionth of the global digital population via the Internet, sell your art on eBay, get paid via PayPal, and become a star inside this very specific network of 5000 people. Technological banes can become technological boons. New needs will arise when humans understand the new technology. Of course there will be turmoil, some economic adjustment will be necessary, and some workers will become unemployed due to technological change, but we should not underestimate the human capacity to react to these changes and shouldn't close our eyes to this aspect of the ongoing digital revolution.

# Economic Growth Increases People's Well-Being

## Richard A. Easterlin

**》** *There is no positive long-term relationship between happiness and a growing GDP. It's time to think about alternatives.*

Economic growth is commonly taken to mean a sustained increase in real GDP per capita. If the per capita production and consumption of goods and services is taken as the fundamental criterion of people's well-being, then the conclusion that naturally follows is that growth and well-being go together.

There are problems, however, with this reasoning. First, the measure of well-being focuses on only the material goods component of people's lives. While one's material living level is important, there are other vital determinants of well-being that are disregarded, such as family life, health, work, and aspirations. Second, and even more important, the judgment of what constitutes well-being is made by an outside observer—the social scientist or statistician—not those being observed. The judgments of outside observers can and do vary widely on the appropriate content of well-being. In contrast, who is better equipped to judge their own well-being than those being observed?

A measure of well-being that does not have these shortcomings and is becoming increasingly accepted by scholars and policy-makers is "life

R.A. Easterlin (✉)
Economics Department, University of Southern California, Los Angeles, CA, USA

© Springer International Publishing AG 2017
B.S. Frey, D. Iselin (eds.), *Economic Ideas You Should Forget,*
DOI 10.1007/978-3-319-47458-8_15

satisfaction" or "happiness," the response, for example, on a ten-point scale to survey questions such as, "In general how satisfied are you with your life?" or "How happy are you these days?" These measures have the advantage that the evaluation of well-being is made by those whose well-being is being assessed and that they reflect the broad range of concerns that occupy people's everyday lives. Questions about the meaningfulness of such self-reports have naturally been raised and led to a thorough vetting. The result has been to affirm their value as measures of well-being, as evidenced by the fact that a number of countries have now embarked on the official collection of self-reported well-being as a potential guide to policy.

Over the past half century, data on happiness have accumulated for a growing number of countries worldwide, making it possible to examine how growth and well-being are actually related. The relationship turns out to differ depending on whether one is looking at short-term fluctuations or long-term trends. In the short run—the cyclical relationship—GDP and happiness go up and down together. During the Great Recession, for example, happiness in the United States collapsed as the economy contracted and then recovered as GDP turned upward. But over the long run—the trend relationship—countries with more rapid economic growth do not experience a greater increase in happiness. Indeed, in the United States, the trend in happiness has been flat for over seven decades, a period in which real GDP per capita more than tripled. Even more spectacular, China's life satisfaction was no higher in 2010 than in 1990, despite an unprecedented fourfold multiplication of real GDP per capita in only two decades. There are some scholars who claim to find that happiness trends upward along with GDP, but they are confusing the positive short-term relationship with the nil long-term relationship. The absence of a long-term relationship suggests that it is time to reconsider the long-held belief that economic growth increases human well-being.

# Big Data Predictions Devoid of Theory

Thomas Ehrmann

» The end of theory is a claim often made by pro-
tagonists of big data. This is a dangerous claim.
Without developing theory-based models that can
stand subsequent thorough testing, we will not
learn anything about how the world truly works.

A famous article by Chris Anderson, published in *Wired* in 2008, was titled: "The data deluge makes the scientific method obsolete." Its basic argument asserts that many researchers currently fall for the lure of massive amounts of data combined with applied mathematics, which in effect replace every other tool that might be useful for making sound predictions in science. Following the latter orientation, theories of human behavior results are apparently abandoned, no matter whether such theories are grounded in psychology, sociology, or economics. From Anderson's perspective, it is simply considered not to be interesting anymore to understand the driving forces of why people do what they do. In contrast, observation of human behavior is often (yet, wrongly) assumed to be sufficient, also because one can easily track and measure such behavior and record data on it. Then, given myriads of "reliable" data, the numbers are supposed to speak for themselves.

T. Ehrmann (✉)
University of Muenster, Muenster, Germany

© Springer International Publishing AG 2017                                    **39**
B.S. Frey, D. Iselin (eds.), *Economic Ideas You Should Forget*,
DOI 10.1007/978-3-319-47458-8_16

On the contrary, the "pre-big data" approach has long concentrated on developing testable hypotheses, derived from some sort of well-founded theory. Based on these hypotheses, models are subsequently empirically tested, and these tests confirm or falsify models intended to explain how the world functions. With massive data, powerful computers and data mining algorithms, today there are business experts and even *economists* who believe that the "hypothesize, model and finally test approach" to predictions is rapidly becoming obsolete. For example, Erik Brynjolfsson and Lynn Wu (2015) stress the power of big data: Using data from search engines, they propose that these data provide a simple but an accurate way to predict future business activities. Applying their data to predict housing market trends, they find that their housing search index is strongly predictive of future housing market sales and prices. They conclude that "nanoeconomic" data will transform predictions in many markets and will have a very strong impact on business strategy and consumer decision-making.

Taking these developments into account, what will the future hold? We can already find numerous articles in economic journals that do not rely on a theory and testable hypotheses any longer but simply go for letting the computer find correlations in some kind of predefined direction. Such articles are titled, for example, "handedness and earnings" or "beautiful parents have more daughters," and they demonstrate some intuitively "interesting" (though not necessarily "interesting" from a scientific point of view) effect and thereby, sometimes make it to the newspaper headlines.

In a brilliant study on astrological signs and health, Peter Austin and others (2006) illustrated how multiple "hypotheses" testing (or in the data mining world, correlation checks) can be used to produce associations with no theoretical (here, no clinical) plausibility. In their study, they used automated methods for data mining to detect apparently significant associations in a large dataset. They found that persons born under the sign of Leo had a significantly higher probability of gastrointestinal hemorrhage, while Sagittarians had a significantly higher probability of humerus fracture compared to all other signs combined.

Where is the specific risk of data mining approaches for economics? Let us assume that we can come up with 1000 "hypotheses" (or rather, supposed correlations), of which, a priori, a mere 100 should hold true. The probability for false positive and false negative shall be 10 % and 20 %. So even a thoroughly carried out analysis will lead to an error ratio, the ratio of reported significant findings that are false, of $(1 - 80/170) = 53$ %. Now, the more powerful computers we have and the more data we get, the more "hypotheses"/"correlations" can be tested: Consider testing 100,000 "hypotheses" or checking 100,000 correlations, assuming a still (in fact, very high) a priori probability of being true of 1 %. Using the assumptions from above, we get an error ratio of $1 - (800/10700) = 92.5$ %!

In summary, without developing theory-based models that can stand up to subsequent thorough testing, we will not learn anything about how the world truly works.

The only thing we will know, however, is that the error rate of data mining is a priori exceptionally high.

# References

Austin PC, Mamdani MM, Juurlink DN, Hux JE. Testing multiple statistical hypotheses resulted in spurious associations: a study of astrological signs and health. J Clin Epidemiol. 2006 Sep;59(9):964–9. Epub 2006 Jul 11.

Lynn Wu, Erik Brynjolfsson. The Future of Prediction: How Google Searches Foreshadow Housing Prices and Sales. Chapter in NBER book Economic Analysis of the Digital Economy (2015), Avi Goldfarb, Shane Greenstein, and Catherine Tucker, editors (p. 89–118).

# Government Debts Are a Burden on Future Generations

## Reiner Eichenberger

**》** *Present debts reduce the future attractiveness of a jurisdiction. Hence, future property prices decrease, which is anticipated in today's markets and reflected in present property prices. Consequently, present debts are a burden not on future generations but on present property owners.*

The idea that government debts are a burden on future generations is not only dominant in the public and political discourse but also consistent with the academic economic perspective. According to the Barro-Ricardo equivalence theorem, the debt burden remains with the present generation only under highly restrictive assumptions which usually do not hold, most importantly, the assumption of perfect intergenerational altruism between present and future citizens. While it can be argued that extensive altruism may exist between parents and their children, many citizens have no children. Moreover, increasing migration between jurisdictions decreases intergenerational altruism

R. Eichenberger (✉)
University of Fribourg, Fribourg, Switzerland

CREMA – Center for Research in Economics, Management and the Arts,
Zurich, Switzerland
e-mail: reiner.eichenberger@unifr.ch

© Springer International Publishing AG 2017
B.S. Frey, D. Iselin (eds.), *Economic Ideas You Should Forget*,
DOI 10.1007/978-3-319-47458-8_17

as it shrinks the probability that the present citizens' children will live in the same jurisdictions as their parents.

However, these arguments are rendered obsolete by capitalization of government debts into property prices. As government debts have to be served or repaid, they are a constraint on future politics. The higher the present government net debts of a jurisdiction are, the higher its future taxes have to be or the fewer government services can be provided in the future. Thus, present debts reduce the future attractiveness of a jurisdiction. This induces future property prices to decrease, which is anticipated in today's markets and reflected in present property prices. Consequently, present debts are a burden not on future generations but on present property owners.

What is the extent of the capitalization of government debts? The mechanism of debt capitalization is closely related to tax capitalization. The tax burden is shifted between factors of production depending on their relative elasticities of supply and demand. Within countries as well as between small open economies, labor and capital are highly mobile across borders, i.e., their supply is highly elastic. In contrast, the supply of land is quite or even totally inelastic. Consequently, land bears the full burden of local taxes. The same applies to local debts. The more mobile capital and labor are, the more fully land and its present owners bear the full debt burden. Thus, federalism is a protector of future generations and maximizes intergenerational welfare. While it prevents the present inhabitants from exploiting future generations, it has also protected the present generation from having been exploited by bygone generations.

In order to empirically test debt capitalization, data on gross government debts as well as government assets are needed. While such data is usually not available, Switzerland represents an exception as municipalities have been providing account balances that reflect their debts and assets for decades. David Stadelmann and I have extensively tested debt capitalization in the 171 municipalities of the Canton of Zurich for which also high-quality housing price data is available. The results are striking: Municipal debts capitalize largely if not fully into property prices, and it is the present generation that carries the debt burden. However, this is only true with high mobility of capital and labor such as it exists among lower-level jurisdictions or in small open economies. If the right to issue debts is relegated to the central level of large countries or even to the international level, e.g., to the EU, each generation can live at the expense of future generations.

# Public Spending Reduces Unemployment

## Lars P. Feld

> **»** *It is a nice idea but too simplistic and too general: public spending reduces unemployment. We should focus on what policy makers concretely can do in the particular situation of a country.*

Since Keynes's General Theory, many people believe in the simple effects of expansionary fiscal policy that public spending reduces unemployment. In the continuing debate about the best policies to cope with the euro crisis, many observers think that finance ministers in Europe should increase spending and that Europe needs a fiscal stimulus. This is too simplistic. The effects of fiscal stimulus depend heavily on the particular situation of a country, e.g., whether it is highly indebted or not. Sometimes, higher public spending even increases in employment.

This argument follows simple principles of economics reasoning. First, there are the statistical identities. Calculating gross domestic product (GDP), government spending enters at cost. Each dollar spent by definition increases GDP by that dollar. Fiscal consolidation therefore necessarily reduces GDP. Second, spending public money directly increases employment, e.g., by hiring additional public employees or by public procurement. Third, those salaries of public employees or the revenue of firms conducting public works flow back

L.P. Feld (✉)
Albert-Ludwigs-University of Freiburg, Freiburg im Breisgau, Germany

© Springer International Publishing AG 2017
B.S. Frey, D. Iselin (eds.), *Economic Ideas You Should Forget*,
DOI 10.1007/978-3-319-47458-8_18

into the economy, because individuals and firms consume, invest, and, thus, spend. This process allows for multipliers of fiscal policy. Since the Great Recession, the debate about the size of these multipliers has intensified.

The wide range of multipliers in the literature underlines that such arguments are too simplistic. If a country is close to defaulting, additional public spending will lead to higher unemployment. If such a country can get someone to lend to it at all, the additional indebtedness can tick its financial situation to bankruptcy. No private investor will expand its production and hire employees in such a situation. This argument still holds, while less dramatically, whenever countries are only highly indebted. The expansionary impulse of a fiscal stimulus decreases, perhaps even turns negative, the more private consumers and investors must expect to face high contributions in ensuing consolidation processes. This mechanism has become famous as the non-Keynesian effect of fiscal consolidation. It mainly works through expectations of market participants but also via uncertainty in financial markets.

Between these two polar cases of Keynesian and non-Keynesian effects, there is a wide range of outcomes. Whether public spending reduces unemployment depends on the particular situation of a country, on the situation of other countries involved in trade with that country, on the state of its public finances, on the situation in financial markets, on the level of refinancing costs, on the willingness of taxpayers to finance additional public spending, and on the usefulness of the actual spending programs, just to name a few. Anything goes. Therefore, the contention that public spending reduces unemployment does not hold. We should forget about this simple economic idea and analyze what fiscal policy makers can concretely do in a particular situation of a country.

The resulting skepticism does not argue for more vs. less or big vs. small government. Some countries, e.g., within Scandinavia, organize big government comparably efficiently. Public administration works well, the government spends money for programs that its citizens want, thereby increasing taxpayers' willingness to pay taxes, and automatic stabilizers serve their macroeconomic purposes. Other countries with big government, e.g., France, are in a worse situation.

Similarly, the skepticism regarding discretionary fiscal policy does not mean that the whole idea must be discarded. In a severe economic downturn or a liquidity trap, fiscal stimuli provide important economic impulses. The general recommendation to governments must be, however, to reduce their public-debt-to-GDP ratios and keep them low in order to be able to provide the necessary fiscal stimulus when it is necessary to stimulate the economy.

# The Capital Asset Pricing Model

## Pablo Fernandez

>> *The CAPM is a very popular model. That should not stop us from forgetting about it. Simple reasoning can do the same trick.*

The capital asset pricing model (CAPM) is an absurd model—its assumptions *and* its predictions/conclusions have no basis in the real world.

With the vast amount of information and research that has been done, it is quite clear that the CAPM does not "explain facts or events," nor does it "describe the past, present, or future state of something."

The use of CAPM is also a source of litigation: many professors, lawyers, etc. get hefty fees because a vast number of professionals use CAPM instead of common sense to calculate the required return to equity. Users of the CAPM make many illogical errors in valuing companies, accepting or rejecting investment projects, evaluating fund performance, pricing goods and services in regulated markets, calculating value creation, and the list goes on.

P. Fernandez (✉)
University of Navarra, Pamplona, Spain

© Springer International Publishing AG 2017
B.S. Frey, D. Iselin (eds.), *Economic Ideas You Should Forget*,
DOI 10.1007/978-3-319-47458-8_19

**47**

## Main Predictions of the CAPM

The CAPM assumptions imply that all investors:

(a) Will always combine a risk-free asset with the market portfolio
(b) Will have the same portfolio of risky assets (the market portfolio)
(c) Will agree on the expected return and expected variance of the market portfolio and every asset
(d) Will agree on the expected MRP and beta of every asset
(e) Will expect returns from their investments according to the betas

## Why Is the CAPM an Absurd Model?

The CAPM is based on numerous unrealistic assumptions. It is true that "all interesting models involve unrealistic simplifications," and while the CAPM does have some assumptions that are convenient simplifications, its other assumptions (especially the homogeneous expectations) are obviously senseless.

None of the CAPM predictions occur in the real world. And still, many professors will affirm that "the CAPM is not testable" or "it is difficult to test the validity." CAPM is a model (a) based on senseless assumptions, and (b) none of its predictions happen in our world. Which other tests do we need to reject it?

## Why Are People then Still Using the CAPM?

In 2009, I surveyed finance professors on the use of CAPM, and while many of them acknowledge that there are problems estimating two ingredients of the CAPM formula (the beta and the market risk premium), they nevertheless continue to use it for several reasons:

- *It* "[h]as received a Nobel Prize in Economics."
- "Fortune 500 firms use the CAPM to estimate their cost of equity."
- "While not perfect, it is used extensively in practice."
- "Beta is simple and it is used in the real world."
- "If one does not use beta then what is there?"
- "No substitution so far. There are no better alternatives."
- "There is no other satisfactory tool in finance."

- "Calculated betas are on the CFA exam."
- "Regulatory practice often requires it."
- "Beta allows you to defend a valuation, impress management, and come across as a finance guru."
- "In consulting, it is essential to fully support your estimates."

Other professors argue that "[they] teach CAPM because it is based on the important concept of diversification and it is an easy recipe for most students." However, think we can teach diversification without the CAPM and, more importantly, business and management (which includes investment and valuation) is about common sense, not about recipes.

Users of the CAPM have made a multitude of errors valuing companies, accepting or rejecting investment projects, evaluating fund performance, pricing goods and services in regulated markets, calculating value creation, and the list goes on.

# Innovation Programs Lead to Innovation

## Gerd Folkers

>> *It is discovery that leads to true innovation, not some innovation programs that combine science with economic targets.*

Gravitational waves are real. Two enormous antenna arms were shaken by an event far away in the universe as one black hole devoured another. And this unimaginably large change in mass created a ripple in space-time. As unbelievable as it is shocking, it is a triumph for a theory that Einstein himself never believed could be empirically verified. Scientists are talking about the emergence of a new physical era.

Meanwhile, the press and political pundits are talking money. The experiment that led to the discovery of ripples in space-time received high praise. Press conferences were called all over the world to discuss the fundamental importance of the findings for our world view—and each ended with unanimous praise for the politicians and administrations that had the courage and perseverance to believe in the science, despite requiring an additional investment of USD 200 million after a decade of failures and silent antennae.

But what constitutes a "failure?" Scientists can never agree on when it is time to bring an experiment to an end. When the money has run out? Or perhaps after 5 years—the time it usually takes to gradually collect the money

G. Folkers (✉)
ETH Zurich, Zurich, Switzerland

© Springer International Publishing AG 2017                    **51**
B.S. Frey, D. Iselin (eds.), *Economic Ideas You Should Forget*,
DOI 10.1007/978-3-319-47458-8_20

for an experiment, after reaching countless targets and milestones and publishing numerous progress reports? After all, no more money will be offered after the final evaluation.

Most scientific experiments allow for an open outcome, and those that don't should rather be ascribed to engineering. In these cases, the findings can be directly exploited—but this is not the case for the majority of science. As Einstein himself experienced as a bitter insult in Berlin, science is very often Dadaist. It would seem absurd to claim that space and time may change as dictated by our equations. This is precisely what happens, yet Einstein was accused of Dadaist science when discussing his theory at a public lecture. And who would ever invest in Dada?

Consequently, it is pointless to discuss investment in research projects and to praise an investment when it results in a new discovery. Scientific discovery is not scalable, and greater investment does not automatically yield a greater return. In the past, even small experiments produced groundbreaking results, like when Louis Pasteur looked into his microscope or Alexander Fleming peered into his fridge. In the first case, the justification of stereochemistry was initially of purely academic interest, while penicillin ultimately proved to be crucial to the outcome of the war. The ability to recognize a different pattern from the hundreds of observers before them justifiably made both scientists famous. And both cases reflect Pasteur's own assertion that "chance favors only the prepared mind," also known as serendipity.

Back to the ripple in space-time, no result would also have been a result, namely, to refute Einstein's theory. To me, at least, this would have been just as exciting as confirming it. However, the antennae could still have been too small to find a positive signal. The size needed to detect anything was always a guess, so the credo was "let's try a bit bigger." What's more, they've grown in size for decades without finding anything—not a good omen for investment. Indeed, return on investment is a useless concept here. Knowledge accrual does not bow to economic pressures, and all the spillover success stories, from the Teflon pan to GPS navigation, came long after their respective experiments had to be justified to the funding committee.

Forget the economy when it comes to real science. Science demands money, dedication, intellectual brilliance, and the ability to see things that others never have. Forget those who approach science with economic targets to secure a patent, become a young millionaire, or strive for fame and fortune in the attention economy. These people produce findings that lead to rare innovations at best. Meanwhile, their other findings languish in libraries until a genuine scientific discovery allows them to be classified.

Innovation programs with 5-year plans and milestones may lead to technical solutions that are commercially viable. However, they rarely produce break-throughs, and the opportunity costs compared to knowledge-driven research are never calculated.

# Factors of Production Are Homogenous Within Categories

Nicolai J. Foss

>> *Economics focuses on a stylized model of the production process and therefore tries to simplify things by homogenizing assumptions. This hinders the understanding of differences in economic organizations and entrepreneurship.*

The drive to somehow reduce the confusing heterogeneity we observe in the world is a strong one. Ancient philosophical discussions of the existence of universals and abstract objects and taxonomic exercises in early biological science reflect this drive, as does the search for fundamental mechanisms that we call theorizing. In economics it is reflected in several homogenizing assumptions. Thus, much discussion in economics has revolved around assumptions about homogeneity, such as the profit maximization debate, the Cambridge capital controversy, and the meaning of the "representative agent." Here I focus on the assumption that factors of production can for many purposes be taken to be homogeneous within categories. To this end, consider capital.

Most of economics (the obvious exception being Austrian economics) implicitly adopt a view of capital as a homogeneous mass. Paul Samuelson called this the "shmoo" view of capital after the "Li'l Abner" cartoon where shmoos are identical creatures, shaped like bowling pins that can transform

N.J. Foss (✉)
Bocconi University, Milan, Italy

© Springer International Publishing AG 2017 **55**
B.S. Frey, D. Iselin (eds.), *Economic Ideas You Should Forget*,
DOI 10.1007/978-3-319-47458-8_21

into any shape. In this view, capital is an infinitely elastic, fully moldable factor that can be substituted costlessly from one production process to another. In a world of shmoo capital, many fundamental economic problems simply evaporate.

Economics focuses on a stylized model of the production process. The firm is a production function that transforms inputs that are, in the basic representation, homogenous within categories (land, labor, and capital) into output. However, if these inputs are identical, within and across firms, we have no explanation for the huge and persistent differences in firm performance that we readily observe. Additionally, in a world of shmoo capital, economic organization is relatively unimportant. If capital assets are pretty much identical, the costs of inspecting, measuring, and monitoring the attributes of productive assets only have to be ascertained once. Markets for capital assets are then devoid of transaction costs. A few basic contractual problems—in particular, principal-agent conflicts—may remain, although workers would all use identical capital assets, which would greatly contribute to reducing the costs of measuring their productivity. Thus, shmoo capital is the handmaiden of the zero-transaction-cost assumption.

While transaction costs would not disappear entirely in such a world, asset ownership would be relatively unimportant. The possibility of specifying all possible uses of an asset significantly reduces the costs of writing complete and contingent contracts between resource owners and entrepreneurs to govern the uses of the relevant assets. Contracts would largely substitute for ownership, leaving the boundary of the firm indeterminate.

Similarly, in a world of shmoo capital, the entrepreneur is unimportant. Entrepreneurs may equilibrate consumer goods markets, but if capital is a single good with only one price, the entrepreneur only has to choose between capital-intensive and labor-intensive production methods (or among types of labor). Decision problems are thus trivialized. This is also is a noncomplex world where decision-makers do not reach the bounds of their rationality.

Similar reasoning applies to other factors of production. While homogenizing assumptions may sometimes be warranted in economics, much progress comes from breaking with them, particularly with respect to understanding economic organization and entrepreneurship.

# Individual Utility Depends Only on Absolute Consumption

Robert Frank

>> *The traditional economic approach states that an individual decline in income is the same as a collective decline by the same proportion. This is not only wrong but sometimes becomes an obstacle for much needed tax increases.*

Traditional economic theory assumes, preposterously, that a person's loss in utility when he alone suffers an income decline is the same as his utility loss when everyone's income declines by the same proportion. In fact, the person's loss in utility is much smaller when everyone's income declines.

Traditional theory's mistake is important because it causes people to overestimate the pain they'll suffer if they pay higher taxes in support of public goods. It is entirely natural to think that if you have less money, you'll find it more difficult to buy the things you want or need. That's because most of the events in life that cause us to have less money—think home fires, job losses, business reverses, divorces, serious illnesses, and the like—are ones that reduce our incomes while leaving the incomes of others unaffected. In such cases, we really do find it more difficult to buy what we want. Only half of the houses are in top-half school districts, for example, so we're less likely to be able to bid

R. Frank (✉)
Cornell University, Ithaca, NY, USA

© Springer International Publishing AG 2017
B.S. Frey, D. Iselin (eds.), *Economic Ideas You Should Forget*,
DOI 10.1007/978-3-319-47458-8_22

successfully on those houses if we have less money relative to others who also want them.

But it is a completely different story when everyone's disposable income goes down at once, as when we all pay higher taxes. Because across-the-board declines in disposable income leave relative purchasing power unaffected, they don't affect the outcomes of the bidding for houses in better school districts.

This is a garden-variety cognitive error. When we try to forecast how an income decline will affect us, we rely on the previous income declines that are most accessible in memory. And since most of the income declines we actually experience leave the incomes of others unchanged, we tend to forecast similar pain when thinking about the possibilities of a tax increase.

This cognitive error reinforces the tax resistance that has made it so difficult to restore our crumbling public infrastructure. Because across-the-board declines in disposable income don't affect relative purchasing power at all, prosperous families could actually pay higher taxes without having to make any painful sacrifices.

# The Relative Price Effect Explains Behavior

Bruno S. Frey

**》** *The "relative price effect" states that when an activity is more highly rewarded its volume and intensity will be increased. In this concept, intrinsic motivation is neglected and hence the danger of a motivation crowding-out effect can occur.*

Economic theory assumes that – as a matter of course – individuals work more and better when they are offered more money. This view is reflected in the first pages of basic textbooks in which a typical supply curve is increasing in monetary compensation. More generally, the "relative price effect" posits that when an activity is more highly rewarded, its volume and intensity will increase. This reaction is based on the assumption that individual preferences are fixed.

Standard economic theory considers only one motivation in individual preference functions: an extrinsic one, in which selfish and rational people are induced to behave in the desired way. Extrinsic incentives may consist of monetary rewards, other material incentives, or in the threat of punishment.

B.S. Frey (✉)
University of Basel, CREMA, Zurich, Switzerland

CREMA – Center for Research in Economics, Management and the Arts, Zurich, Switzerland

© Springer International Publishing AG 2017
B.S. Frey, D. Iselin (eds.), *Economic Ideas You Should Forget*,
DOI 10.1007/978-3-319-47458-8_23

Intrinsic motivation is disregarded. It consists in undertaking an activity because it is satisfying as such or because it follows a corresponding social norm in a noninstrumental way. For instance, a sizeable part of the population undertakes unpaid voluntary work and gives money to charities even if they are not rewarded from outside. Intrinsic motivation is also required in almost all tasks where performance cannot be fully monitored.

The crucial point overlooked by standard economics is that extrinsic and intrinsic motivations interact. When external rewards are increased, intrinsic motivation may be reduced. This is called the *motivation crowding-out effect*. It depends on two conditions: people must have some degree of intrinsic motivation to start with, and the outside intervention by offering money must be felt to be controlling, which will reduce a person's perceived self-determination and self-esteem. When people are compensated for their work, intrinsic motivation is superfluous and will accordingly be replaced partly or fully by extrinsic motivation.

A motivation *crowding-in* effect occurs when an outside intervention raises intrinsic motivation. This is, for instance, the case when an individual receives an award acknowledging good and engaging work.

Motivation crowding effects have been supported by a large number of laboratory, field, and natural experiments, as well as by careful econometric studies.

Crowding-out effects are relevant in many important areas. Some examples are:

- *Labor market,* where in particular the much heralded performance-related pay tends to crowd out intrinsic motivation to the detriment of work content. Employees are taught, and feel, that reaching the goals set by the superiors is all that matters, inducing them to lose interest in the work itself.
- *Natural environment,* where pricing instruments, such as pollution charges, may crowd out environmental morale.
- *Social policy,* where monetary payments may crowd out responsibility for one's own fate.
- *Subsidies,* which may negatively affect intrinsic entrepreneurship, innovation, and creativity.
- *Voluntary work,* where a monetary compensation tends to crowd out the very reason for engaging in that activity.

The evidence is compelling: extrinsic incentives do not always raise performance and may, in important cases, even reduce it. The relative price effect does not function in important areas and under important conditions. The existence of crowding-out and crowding-in effects suggests that individual preferences may shift in a systematic way due to external interventions.

# The Precedence of Exchange over Production

Jetta Frost

**»** *Economic theories of the firm give too little attention to the key differences between production and exchange. It is time to change this.*

With the rising success of the theory of the firm, questions of why firms exist, what determines their boundaries, and how their internal organization is governed have become very important in economics. Interestingly, these issues are still centered in the sphere of exchange. Exchanges and bundles of contracts are objects of governance. What has been overlooked, however, is the sphere of production. The reason for this is the assumption that the production functions of competing firms or alternative institutional arrangements are more or less identical. Yet, giving precedence to exchange has consequences for governing firms.

The production function of firms is usually kept constant and determined exogenously so that it is equally accessible to all competing firms. Different governance mechanisms are always considered in the context of a given technology. This allows for a focus on the allocation and exchange of information, goods, and services. All knowledge that flows into production is transferable. However, this does not encompass a shift from static to dynamic

J. Frost (✉)
School for Business, Economics and Social Sciences, Universität Hamburg, Hamburg, Germany

© Springer International Publishing AG 2017
B.S. Frey, D. Iselin (eds.), *Economic Ideas You Should Forget*,
DOI 10.1007/978-3-319-47458-8_24

efficiency. Many efforts have been made to consider costs of production *and* transaction within the theory of the firm, but this should not distract from the fact that production costs are determined ex ante and do not vary with regard to different transaction modes. Firms are "price-takers" and offer only few differentiable services.

Governing production is influenced by the decision to buy or sell and by making contracts. As such, it becomes subordinate to the exchange relationship. It is assumed that the time for providing the desired services and their quality are determined by the contract structure. All efforts put into organizational governance are determinants of these contractual relationships, because all essential decisions are made when contractual provisions are set. To put it more precisely, they are determinants of the costs that are related to the definition of these contractual relationships.

To sum up, economic theories of the firm give too little attention to the key differences between production and exchange. While the contractual relationship dominates the sphere of exchange, which is characterized by its given set of choices, it is the skills, knowledge, and learning processes brought in by firm members to provide services that are given priority in the sphere of production. So, we should forget the precedence of exchange over production. A knowledge-based or capability-based view could serve as an alternative or at least as a necessary complement, and its emergence has already revitalized the significance of the production sphere. This view takes center stage in the explanation of economic organization and, thus, in a modern theory of the firm. Today, there are a growing number of researchers and practitioners who are convinced that distinctive skills, routines, and knowledge are the most important resources of a firm in establishing dynamic capabilities or competence. A sustainable competitive advantage is not about efficient transaction costs but about knowledge embedded in the organizing principles of firms that cannot be reduced to individuals. The generation, accumulation, and sharing of new knowledge are crucial for a firm, because it cannot simply be duplicated or imitated by other competitors. This requires a shift of perspective from value appropriation to value creation.

# Inequality Reduces Growth

## Clemens Fuest

» *That greater equality would boost growth sounds like an uplifting idea, but it's an illusion. There is no robust—either negative or positive—correlation between the two.*

An economic idea that should be forgotten is the claim that there is a systematic and mechanical negative impact of inequality on growth. Recent studies published by the OECD and the IMF make this claim and conclude that greater equality would boost growth. The OECD calculates, for example, that Germany's gross domestic product (GDP) would now be 6 % higher if inequality had not increased since 1985.

Because economic surveys often emphasize the tension between growth and redistributive objectives, the findings of the OECD's study appear revolutionary—but they are not. The idea is not only much older—dating back at least to the early 1990s—the idea is also wrong. The results constitute a misinterpretation of the existing data and research findings. Firstly, it is not possible to use the correlation between the Gini coefficient and growth in various OECD countries to derive any causal effects of inequality on growth rates. Rather, inequality and growth impact each other and are driven by a number of

C. Fuest (✉)
Ifo Institute—Leibniz Institute for Economic Research at the University of Munich, Munich, Germany

© Springer International Publishing AG 2017
B.S. Frey, D. Iselin (eds.), *Economic Ideas You Should Forget,*
DOI 10.1007/978-3-319-47458-8_25

**63**

factors. These include technological change, economic globalization, and policy initiatives.

Secondly, the survey assumes that inequality and growth in emerging markets such as Turkey and Mexico are correlated in exactly the same way as in highly advanced welfare states such as Sweden and Germany. This makes no sense. And, thirdly, the survey does not examine whether these results remain valid if the baseline year or the analyzed growth phases are varied. The German Council of Economic Experts conducted this analysis in its most recent report and showed that the alleged negative correlation between inequality and growth does not stand up to scrutiny. If the specified parameters are varied, the negative correlation becomes a positive one in some cases.

A further irritation is that the surveys published by the IMF and the OECD contradict each other. Whereas the IMF claims that inequality resulting from ever higher top incomes is bad for growth, the OECD asserts the opposite, stating that top incomes do not affect growth and that low incomes are the problem. At the same time, the OECD concludes that investment in education has no bearing on growth. How exactly it arrived at that result is a mystery.

There is extensive academic literature on the nature of the link between inequality and growth. The consensus finding of this research is that there is no robust correlation—either negative or positive—between the two. This is hardly surprising if we consider the economic transmission channels that link inequality and growth. For example, higher education spending on children from disadvantaged backgrounds can reduce inequality and boost growth. If, on the other hand, a highly advanced welfare state suffers a crisis because redistributive taxes and regulation stifle performance and investment incentives, then one might expect deregulation and tax cuts to raise inequality while also boosting growth.

Examples of the latter are the UK in the 1980s and Sweden in the 1990s. The policies introduced by Margaret Thatcher provided the UK with greater income inequality as well as an economic boom. Sweden in the early 1990s was hit by a severe economic crisis that arose partly from its ballooning welfare state. The country's politicians passed a number of reforms, which boosted the economy while at the same time increasing income inequality.

The aim of economic policy should be to generate growth that benefits all sections of society—not just the wealthy. However, the notion that less inequality automatically produces more growth—and that redistributive policies can thus be stepped up without any consideration for their impact on growth—is pure fantasy and by no means an economic insight on which to base policy.

# Contingent Valuation, Willingness to Pay, and Willingness to Accept

## Victor Ginsburgh

---

**»** *If economists don't know a price of a nonmarket good, they tend to ask consumers about their willingness to pay. Bad idea.*

---

Contingent valuation (CV) and its two arms, or deadly weapons, willingness to pay (WTP) and willingness to accept (WTA), are survey methods that are supposed to measure the value of nonmarket goods and are mainly used by cultural and environmental economists. WTP roughly consists of asking consumers (or producers) how much they are willing to pay to avoid a negative or to accept a positive outcome; WTA goes for compensation and asks how much an agent would like to be paid to accept a negative outcome or to forego a positive one. The two methods lead to different results, although in theory, they should not, which is not the worst that could happen.

The two methods are used in cases where no market prices exist. Assume, for example, that a real estate developer wants to erect a 30-floor building

V. Ginsburgh (✉)
ECHRES, Université libre de Bruxelles, CP 114/04 50, Avenue F. Roosevelt, 1050 Bruxelles, Belgium
e-mail: vginsbur@ulb.ac.be

© Springer International Publishing AG 2017
B.S. Frey, D. Iselin (eds.), *Economic Ideas You Should Forget*,
DOI 10.1007/978-3-319-47458-8_26

between a beautifully snowcapped mountain and the mansions in which you live. There exists no market for a mountain that nobody wants to buy, of course. Question: "How much are you and your neighbors willing to pay the developer to give up his interesting project?" Or, the more difficult question: "How much are you willing to pay to move the mountain and put it between your mansions and the 30-floor building?" If one opts for the second version of the story, one has to be even more careful, since it has been shown that "the assessed value of a public good (in our case the mountain) is demonstrably arbitrary, because WTP for the same good can vary over a wide range depending on whether the good is assessed on its own or embedded as part of a more inclusive package."

Ecologists and economists who care for our environment or our cultural heritage have widely (and wildly) used this method, which could also be mobilized for museums, concerts or concert halls, theaters, radio stations, and a host of other situations, such as oil spills.

And indeed, the method was subject to criticism a long time ago in a report by a panel of 22 famous economists hired by the National Oceanic and Atmospheric Administration (NOAA) after the Exxon Valdez oil spill. The problem is made worse if, as happens quite often, people who are interviewed only have incomplete (or no) information about the goods or services they have to value, or if these goods and services do not yet exist, but are to be created or introduced, such as in the mountain moving example. How should we know how much each of us loses (or how much Alaska lost) after the Exxon Valdez oil spill or how much we would be willing to pay to avoid such a spill? At best we just invent answers, and at worst we give strategic answers or "purchase moral satisfaction."

The report commissioned by the NOAA was very critical, while later on some other economists were rather sanguinary. One of the two papers in question asks whether "some number [is] better than no number." The second paper adds to this by suggesting that contingent valuation is not only "dubious" but is "hopeless" as well. The writer concludes that he does not "expect that proponents and opponents of CV will ever agree. Some bad ideas in economics and econometrics maintain a surprising viability." Proof: In 2011, a compendium of CV, WTP, and WTA included a bibliography containing 7500 entries. And I am sure there is much more 5 years later.

Because, as is the claim of those who come to the rescue of such methods, there is no alternative. . .

# Governments Must Reduce Budget Deficits

### Michael Graff

**》** *The "night watchman state" has won wide support in recent years. Governments should reduce their budget deficits, as they are never sustainable. This is not in line with the principles of debt financed investment; investment yielding positive social return in the future should be debt financed in the present.*

One of the most consequential ideas in contemporary economics is that governments must reduce budget deficits—preferably to zero. A strict version recommends banning government borrowing once and for all, whereas a more moderate one aims at a balanced budget over the business cycle, where borrowing is admissible during economic downswings, conditional on commitments to budget surpluses of equal magnitudes during upswings.

Amazingly, while this reasoning is based on beliefs rather than economic theory, it is widely accepted among academic economists, politicians, and the public. Formerly reserved for bold supporters of a *night watchman state* (juridical system, armed forces), the moderate version is now regarded as the culmination of fiscal wisdom, even by those who otherwise argue in favour of

M. Graff (✉)
KOF Swiss Economic Institute, ETH Zurich, Zurich, Switzerland

© Springer International Publishing AG 2017
B.S. Frey, D. Iselin (eds.), *Economic Ideas You Should Forget*,
DOI 10.1007/978-3-319-47458-8_27

active government intervention. Consequently, a growing number of national and local government bodies are enshrining this recommendation in the form of so-called *debt brakes* into their legislation.

What are the claims to support such policies? Firstly, government borrowing may compete with private borrowing, depleting loanable funds and driving interest rates up, thereby *crowding out* private investment and/or consumption, substituting it with government expenditure. Secondly, the cumulated budget deficits of the past are the present debt, which is the real concern. Thirdly, some economists view governments as mostly, if not entirely, acting in the self-interest of its officials, with the result of undesirable government spending due to cronyism or the need to secure the public's support in elections or to keep them from rioting. Hence, binding rules to restrict government spending are called for.

For the zero tolerance proponents, crowding out is categorically undesirable, based on the conviction that private expenditure is preferable to *any* government spending beyond what is required to maintain the *night watchman state*, as individuals know best what is good for them. Without deficits, debt cannot accumulate, and the story ends here. The more sophisticated recommendations are based on the evident fact that an ever-growing government debt, in excess of GDP, will at some stage become unsustainable. Yet, permanent budget deficits are perfectly in line with a constant debt to GDP ratio, although the tolerable limit is disputable. However, both zero tolerance and debt brakes restrict net government borrowing to zero in the long run. Positive nominal GDP growth will then drive any debt to GDP ratio asymptotically down to zero and even the apparently more moderate position would yield the same result. While it allows for some Keynesian business cycle fine-tuning, the zero debt outcome effectively bans governments from borrowing for investment purposes.

Thus, what is regarded as perfectly fine and desirable for private business, to borrow if the expected return exceeds the interest rate, should not apply to the government. The long-standing *golden rule of finance* stipulates that all potential government investment yielding a positive social return in the future in excess of the lending rate should be debt financed. This will benefit the present generation, will increase what future generations inherit in terms of infrastructure and social and cultural capital, and will exceed the government debt they will have to serve. Who would complain or turn down such an inheritance? Only those who hold the misanthropic belief that governments are inevitably incompetent or corrupt.

# Reach for Your Dream

## Allan Guggenbühl

>> *Economic rules suggest that you should always reach for the maximum, for more growth. This ignores human psychology. Life does not get better all the time; perpetual growth is an illusion.*

Humans share many traits with animals. They communicate, like dolphins do; they grieve, as we know from chimpanzees; they create communities like elephants; and they tend to their children, similar to tigers. So where is the *decisive* difference? According to Suddendorf, we humans are capable of *mental travels*. We create scenes and situations in our heads, which have *no* connection with our current situation. We imagine that we are enjoying a sunny day on a Caribbean island, while in reality we are sitting in a stuffy subway. The more important difference, though, is that the images in our heads have *power* over us! They influence our decisions and distract us from our ordinary duties and routines. We become dissatisfied and strive for something different. History is full of events, where humans departed from their common grounds, dared to confront unforeseeable challenges and dangers, because they pursued an imagined scene. Sometimes they succeeded; oftentimes they failed miserably. This is not only the case for individuals, like the unlucky Franz Reichelt, who in 1912 was convinced he could parachute from the Eiffel Tower wearing a

A. Guggenbühl (✉)
Institute for Conflict Management, Zurich, Switzerland

© Springer International Publishing AG 2017
B.S. Frey, D. Iselin (eds.), *Economic Ideas You Should Forget*,
DOI 10.1007/978-3-319-47458-8_28

self-made jump jacket and leapt to his death. Whole nations have experienced catastrophes because of delusional projects. Scotland went bankrupt and had to join the Union, because their bold Darien adventure in the jungles of Panama failed, evaporating their expensive dream of a Scottish colony and leaving more than two thousand Scots to perish. Dreams impel humans to leave their comfort zone and make irrational decisions. If they are lucky, the outcomes are great discoveries and inventions. The snag is that the satisfaction for having reached a goal wanes and the old discontent emerges again.

Reaching for a dream can be a dangerous strategy. Repeatedly, people were inundated by visions of power, wealth, and perpetual delight. It enabled them to break loose, rebel, and initiate change. Christianity, which originated as one of numerous sects and sprouted in the margins of the Roman Empire, appealed to thousands of miserable subjects crammed into Rome. They sacrificed themselves for the promise of paradise, possibly during their lifetime! In contrast to the polytheistic Mithras religion, Christianity had a promise to offer. Paradise was an escape route from slavery. One reason the Roman Empire crumbled is because it lost its vigor to more powerful images.

Have we learned anything? Our tendency to fall for fantastic ideas prevails. The wording is different. Instead of dreaming of paradise, we rely on daring economic strategies. If there is a lack of growth, let the Federal Reserve Bank or ECB print money and lend it to banks, and this money is gratis. No worries! The instigated economic boom will reimburse the debts. If there are no immediate results, print more! The promised growth must come! A fantasy is understood *concretely*, just like the early Christians believed in the immediate arrival of paradise. In the meantime, the deficits have reached astronomical heights: $16 trillion in the United States, £1.56 trillion in the UK, and 345 billion € in Greece. These debt will *never* be paid back, because it is unthinkable that the economy will suddenly grow at a miraculous rate. The consequences for national economies will be disastrous.

The problem with this economic idea is that it ignores the human psychology. We have ups and downs; depression alternates with happiness. Life does not get better *all* the time; dark moments belong to our existence. *Perpetual* growth is an illusion. Just as we humans have phases of decline, economies will dwindle. Instead of envisaging constant growth—the myth of our times—we need to create a culture, where success and failure take turns and we are prepared to relinquish part of our wealth, a culture where growth and decline is the normal course of life. But maybe that is an illusion, too.

# The EU's Competiveness Authority

### Beat Gygi

**»** *The European Union tries to improve member countries' competitiveness by introducing a competitiveness authority. That's a bad idea, and it's closely related to the lack of checks and balances in the EU's system.*

The European Union is in a bad state. The economic performance of the Euro area and the competitiveness of many member countries are far below the ambitious plans presented 10 years ago. Further, there is a growing divergence across the Euro area. The monetary union has led to serious conflicts and tensions within Europe, responsibilities have become vague, redistribution between member countries increased, necessary reforms are postponed in many member states, and national debts are huge and rising—often in countries with already high unemployment rates, slow growth, and poor economic prospects. The EU needs more economic growth, confidence, and competition.

In order to "correct" the divergence in the EU and give a new boost to the convergence process, the leaders of the EU launched the "The Five Presidents' Report" in 2015. Jean-Claude Juncker (president of the European Commission), Donald Tusk (president of the European Council), Jeroen Dijsselbloem

B. Gygi (✉)
Weltwoche, Zurich, Switzerland

© Springer International Publishing AG 2017
B.S. Frey, D. Iselin (eds.), *Economic Ideas You Should Forget*,
DOI 10.1007/978-3-319-47458-8_29

(president of the Eurogroup), Mario Draghi (president of the European Central Bank, ECB), and Martin Schulz (president of the European Parliament) presented a road map to "develop concrete mechanisms for stronger economic policy coordination, convergence, and solidarity" aiming at "better economic governance."

They foresee actions on four fronts: (1) working toward a "genuine economic union," wherein each country should do its homework in structural reforms, economic efficiency, and competitiveness; (2) working toward a "financial union" by completing the banking union and accelerating the capital markets union; (3) working toward a "fiscal union," leading to coordination and stabilization of national fiscal policies; and lastly, (4) working toward a "political union" by providing a general foundation for an increasing integration of political decision-making.

Now to the point: What would be the best way to improve member countries' competitiveness? Most economists would say this: more competition. No, say the five presidents. Their solution is competitiveness authorities! This may sound almost like competition but is a very different approach. The presidents want to create a national body in charge of tracking performance and policies concerning competitiveness in each country. Surveillance should help to prevent economic divergence and push forward the necessary reforms at the national level. What will such competitive authorities do in reality? They will try to coordinate their work, avoid conflicts with their governments, mollify existing contrasts between countries, establish administrative rules and benchmarks based on average performance, help low performers excuse themselves, and produce mediocre results—just as it was already the case with the Maastricht criteria. The competitiveness authority is an economic idea you should forget.

The real problem is elsewhere: Why do the five presidents so closely cooperate in pushing forward EU integration? The five persons represent five top EU institutions that should in fact control each other, respectively; it should be a system of checks and balances. But the presidents are five buddies fighting as an interest group for their own common goal: EU integration at any price—including Mario Draghi, who moved the so-called independent central bank into the political center of the EU. Five presidents as five friends—an economic idea you should forget!

# Say's Law

## Jochen Hartwig

» Say's Law states that aggregate production neces-sarily creates an equal quantity of aggregate demand. Forget about that. The law ignores the characteristics of money as a store of value.

Say's Law states that aggregate supply necessarily creates an equal amount of aggregate demand. It is the cornerstone of supply-side economics. Say's Law is an economic idea you should forget because it implies a view of money that is untenable. Every textbook tells you that money acts as a medium of exchange and as a store of value, but Say's Law reduces money to the former. It implies that money income must be spent. Aggregate production consists of consumption goods and investment goods. Say's Law would hold if the income not spent on consumption goods must be spent on investment goods, in which case, produced income (supply) would always equal spent income (demand). Hence Say's Law is the flip side of the loanable funds doctrine, which also implies that total money income must be spent. The income not spent on consumption goods is saved, and since it is irrational to forfeit interest income according to the loanable funds doctrine, savings must be spent on interest-

J. Hartwig (✉)
Technische Universität Chemnitz, Chemnitz, Germany

KOF Swiss Economic Institute, ETH Zurich, Zurich, Switzerland

© Springer International Publishing AG 2017                                    **73**
B.S. Frey, D. Iselin (eds.), *Economic Ideas You Should Forget*,
DOI 10.1007/978-3-319-47458-8_30

bearing loanable funds, which are emitted by firms in order to finance investment spending. When the economy is in a situation where the desire to save is high and the desire to invest is low—probably due to high interest rates—aggregate demand for consumption and investment goods can be lower than the output of these goods. But at the same time, there would be an excess demand for loanable funds, which would depress the interest rate until equilibria in both the goods and the loanable funds markets are established.

This line of argument collapses if money can be used as a proper store of value. In other words, Say's Law collapses when money can be hoarded. If excess savings do not affect the interest rate in the way described in the loanable funds doctrine, then an excess supply of money can persist. This also has interesting consequences for the theory of employment. Due to hoarding, money becomes scarcer in relation to goods and services, resulting in a rise in its own price or, put differently, a decline in commodity prices. This means that the real wage rises over and above the rate that precipitated the labor demand decisions of the entrepreneurs at the point in time when they decided how many goods to supply. It follows then that entrepreneurs will only make their decisions on how many workers to employ in the "labor market" (using the "labor demand curve") if money can only serve as a medium of exchange. However, if money can be hoarded, it would be quite foolish for entrepreneurs to make employment decisions disregarding the expectations for aggregate demand, because they could miss the profit-maximizing level of production or even make losses if they did.

Why then is money hoarded? Why is it used as a store of value? According to Keynes's theory of liquidity preference, money is used to guard against fundamental uncertainty. Interest is a reward for waiving liquidity—or for waiving the utility that the possession of money conveys. The more anxious people are, the higher must be the reward to make them part with their money (i.e., the interest rate). The recent financial crisis and the "Euro crisis" provide ample empirical evidence in their aftermaths for the nexus between uncertainty, liquidity preference of individuals and banks, and the rise of interest rates in all places not considered to be safe havens.

# Boundedness of Rationality

## Jürg Helbling

>> *Homo economicus has been buried; we know that. However, rational choice still has its explanatory power, and rationality is not bounded: If an actor's choice appears to be nonrational, this is because the observer's model is incomplete.*

Criticizing the model of *homo economicus* is like killing a corpse. Though its assumptions seem to be necessary for the mathematical modeling of efficient markets, they are nevertheless unrealistic and too far from the reality of real people, as Herbert Simon and others have convincingly demonstrated.

Actors behave strategically and have a certain capacity for conscious foresight. They also have some knowledge and understanding of the world around them. However, actors, ranking expected outcomes, are subjected to various cognitive restrictions, as Simon has shown. Their information about options and outcomes is limited, as is their information about what other actors might do. The time horizon of their decision-making is also limited: Actors are shortsighted and decide myopically. Also the actors' computational capacities are limited: Even if all information were available, it would still be impossible to calculate all the possible pros and cons of all the options (including their probabilities). Real actors do not incessantly calculate costs and benefits of

J. Helbling (✉)
University of Lucerne, Lucerne, Switzerland

© Springer International Publishing AG 2017
B.S. Frey, D. Iselin (eds.), *Economic Ideas You Should Forget*,
DOI 10.1007/978-3-319-47458-8_31

options, but rather behave according to conventions or frames, which have turned out to be successful in similar situations in the past. Simon's is a convincing model of rational choice. The only problem is that the "bounded ness" of rationality seems to imply a deficit of rationality. However, (instrumental) rationality refers to the relation between means and ends and not to the amount of information actors possess. Less informed actors may opt for a risk-avoiding maximin strategy rather than a maximizing strategy, but the cognitive limitations do not render actors' decisions less rational or even irrational.

In a similar vein, behavioral economists such as Tversky, Kahneman, and Thaler have identified a large number of "anomalies" or "deviations" from the standard model of the *homo economicus*. However, as convincing as their experiments may be and as influential their theoretical insights are, they only pose an argument against the model of *homo economicus*, not against rational choice as such. Their findings are not "anomalies," but seem to be compatible with a more realistic model of strategic actors. Due to institutional norms and rules, which provide a long-term perspective, actors tend to behave less myopically. Institutions constrain human action but also allow for collective action, i.e., cooperation, and help to overcome the incentives to defect.

Economists should not believe in the usefulness of further differentiation of psychological properties and cognitive limitations of actors, but rather should address the noncognitive constraints of human action, i.e., the economic, political, and cultural systems and institutions that constitute the incentives to which actors react. The distribution of (economic, political, and cultural) capital and assets may explain the differences between actors (firms) in terms of market and bargaining power in general. The actors' positions in social space may explain their range of options, the means to pursue their ends and their interests. However, in any case, rationality is not "bounded": If an actor's choice appears to be suboptimal or even nonrational, the observer's model must be incomplete or false, i.e., other purposes such as political (power) or cultural gains (reputation) rank higher in the actor's preferential hierarchy than economic goals.

# Rational Expectations

## David F. Hendry

>> *Forget about rational expectations. Every location shift, such as the recent financial crisis or smaller crises, will make the expectations formation by rational expectations obsolete.*

The concept of a 'rational expectation' (RE), defined as the conditional expectation of next period's outcome, given all relevant information today and assuming a known distribution, should be forgotten despite its widespread use in economics to model how agents form expectations about future outcomes. This critique applies most forcefully to 'present value' calculations involving many future periods. Elementary textbook proofs that the conditional expectation is an unbiased, minimum variance predictor rely on the unstated assumption that the distributions involved remain constant. However, unanticipated shifts of distributions occur intermittently—and far too often to pretend that they do not. Conditional expectations fail to be unbiased or minimum variance predictors in our wide-sense non-stationary world. The financial crisis is just the largest of the most recent shifts, but many smaller unanticipated changes also occur (Uber, driverless cars, Airbnb, Brexit, etc. were all largely unexpected until they occurred). History is replete with

D.F. Hendry (✉)
Institute for New Economic Thinking at the Oxford Martin School, University of Oxford, Oxford, UK

© Springer International Publishing AG 2017
B.S. Frey, D. Iselin (eds.), *Economic Ideas You Should Forget,*
DOI 10.1007/978-3-319-47458-8_32

examples of distributional shifts both large and small. The most pernicious form of shift is when the previous mean of a distribution changes unexpectedly to a new value, called a location shift. After every location shift, the mean outcome for every variable affected will differ systematically from the so-called 'rational expectation'. It would therefore be irrational to use such an expectations-formation device. Supposed 'learning mechanisms' that enable economic agents to form expectations that converge to the conditional expectation also fail in processes with unanticipated location shifts, as many similar shifts can be generated by very different underlying changes. After the shift, large data samples would be needed to infer what shifted, assuming nothing else changes in the meantime.

'Dynamic stochastic general equilibrium' (DSGE) models are destroyed by collateral damage from unanticipated shifts of distributions, since their mathematical foundations become invalid—Fubini's theorem is correct, but the law of iterated expectations fails when distributions shift. Today's expectation of tomorrow's conditional expectation given today's information is then not equal to tomorrow's unconditional expectation. Thus, DSGEs are the most susceptible of all model forms to the Lucas critique as they are intrinsically nonstructural from their very derivation. Moreover, there is no 'equilibrium' in any useful sense; rather, we must live with a succession of dynamic disequilibria to which economic agents continually need to adapt. Agents must change their plans when they go awry and market clearing is not a sufficient condition for 'equilibrium'. Rather, robust methods to correct errors are essential for agents and empirical economic models to recover from past mistakes—failing to do so will lead to systematic forecast failure. Location shifts not only wreak havoc with DSGE-type models but also with any empirical model that does not take non-constancy into account, as was seen following the financial crisis. Modern methods of indicator saturation can model such shifts, and robust forecasting devices can replace RE to represent how agents form non-exploitable expectations.

# Letting Insolvent Banks Fail

Gerard Hertig

> **»** *Letting insolvent banks fail sounds like a good idea. But it's not. It would be more efficient to limit resolution to selected situations.*

It is commonly accepted that insolvent banks should be subject to bankruptcy (or, to use today's terminology, resolution). More specifically, when a bank's assets are worth less than its debts, it should *die*. In practical terms, a resolution takes the form of a restructuring performed over a weekend and under the supervision of a judge. Potential acquirers bid for the bank's assets (and often some of its debt), allowing a *new bank* to open for business on Monday morning. The *old bank*'s equity holders and, to a lesser degree, its unsecured creditors swallow the losses when capital is wiped out and the debt is not fully covered by the proceeds of the resolution.

There are, however, generally recognized exceptions to this resolution rule. One exception has to do with externalities. If a bank is very large, resolution is often not practicable without causing havoc within the banking sector or even across the economy. In this situation, failure is normally dealt with by way of a governmental bailout, with the state either nationalizing the bank or becoming a significant shareholder. Another exception targets situations where it is the liquidity of a bank's assets rather than their intrinsic value that causes

G. Hertig (✉)
ETH Zurich, Zurich, Switzerland

B.S. Frey, D. Iselin (eds.), *Economic Ideas You Should Forget*,
DOI 10.1007/978-3-319-47458-8_33

problems. This is normally dealt with via state deposit guarantees. Knowing that they will get their money back, depositors' incentives to transfer their funds to other banks are reduced. As a result, liquidity issues are unlikely to arise in the first place, which in turn minimizes the number of bank failures and the resulting costs for taxpayers.

It would, however, be more efficient to make the exception the rule—and limit resolution to select situations. In past decades, the vast majority of bank resolutions had to do with smaller banks and occurred in financial crisis situations. In such an environment, the expected cost of resolution due to not bailing out failing banks is likely to be higher than the expected cost of bailing out these same banks. More specifically, it has been empirically shown that if the US government had decided to bail out most or even all the 350 (smaller) banks that were resolved in the wake of the 2007–2008 credit crisis, US taxpayers would have been saved billions of US$.

To be sure, converting the rule into the exception does not mean that failing banks should always be bailed out. This would raise moral hazard issues, as banks would take on more risk than they would in an efficient world, without having to suffer the consequences. But, as a quick look at bank failure data clearly shows, very few banks fail in good times. Most banks fail in the context of financial crises, which are hard to foresee and even harder to time. Making bailouts the rule rather than the exception for such extreme events is unlikely to result in moral hazard and inefficient risk-taking.

On the contrary, putting an end to the asymmetric bailout treatment of larger vs. smaller banks may prove efficient. Moreover, it is likely to result in a more diversified allocation of risk-taking, with smaller banks not being at a disadvantage when it comes to significant drops in asset prices. At the same time, a generalized bailout approach may well mitigate the too-big-to-fail issue, as there will be fewer reasons for small banks' counterparties to flock to safe ground and large banks.

# Pleasantville Politics: Selecting Politicians According to Ability

## Bruno Heyndels

> **»** *Selecting politicians according to ability is hardly possible and even less sustainable or desirable. So, don't bother.*

Assume a community that needs politicians. They might not be *desperately* needed, just: needed. Now consider the type of politicians. You may want to select the most empathic ones, the most committed, the most funny, the best-looking, or just the most able. Before you claim that the latter option is by far—and self-evidently—superior, think twice. Selecting politicians according to their ability may turn out to be impossible. And if it were possible, it may not be sustainable. And if it were sustainable, it is most likely to be undesirable. So, we shouldn't bother.

**Impossible**: Consider the world being led by the most able. What would this imply? To start with, we would not need elections anymore. They could be replaced by an exam to be taken by those running for office. A more market-conform solution might be to attract able politicians by offering them higher wages. This has been shown to work. Still, able politicians have been found not to be as committed as their "bad" colleagues. They turn out to be only human after all.

B. Heyndels (✉)
The Vrije Universiteit Brussel, Ixelles, Belgium

B.S. Frey, D. Iselin (eds.), *Economic Ideas You Should Forget*,
DOI 10.1007/978-3-319-47458-8_34

Note that we assumed away the difficulty of defining "ability." If you select 100 m runners to represent your country in the Olympics, the definition is clear: Able runners run fast. Selecting players for your national soccer team may be more difficult, as a wide variety of skills are needed. Still, a 90 min soccer game is by far more predictable than political life over a span of 4 or 6 years. You would need a *highly* able coach (elite) to make the selection. And, yes, you may well want to assume this to be the case, for convenience.

The issue is that convenience may not survive outside the economic model, not even on average, not by far. As a result, a system in which politicians are selected according to ability is unlikely to be found in the real world. As economists, we may still want to insist on assuming that it does.

**Unsustainable**: If we assume that selecting the most able politician is possible, it should be noted that substituting elections by expert selection implies that citizens do not have to bother with politics anymore. This tends to be a good way of making sure that they do. If the ballot voice is not an option, alternatives will be considered. That is, as long as we cannot assume away that citizens have opinions, they can be expected to (want and) express them. People might question whether the officially declared "able" persons leading their community are really as able as they are claimed to be. This might be a fertile breeding ground for apathy, alienation, or even revolution. Some time ago, a Berlin wall fell as a consequence of this apathy, alienation, and revolution.

Further, in our alternative model where able politicians are attracted through high wages and perks, sustainability is an issue. The mechanism implies a crowding out of ability from the private sector. A positive net effect is not guaranteed. Even worse, to the extent that ability in private and public sector differs, attracting "good" politicians through higher wages may crowd out ability in *both* sectors. One doesn't form a good national soccer team by attracting players from among the country's best piano players.

**Undesirable**: Assuming that political leaders *can* be selected according to ability and that citizens *do* think this to be a good idea, is this then our Utopia? Well, I do not know. Political perfection may just be like a jazz concert with a guarantee of no false notes. Honestly, I do not know if this is the Pleasantville-type world in which any of us would like to live.

# The Axioms of Revealed Preference

## John Kay

> **»** *Forget about the axioms of revealed preference, now in use under the label of consistency. There is no objective means of defining whether two situations are in fact the same or are different. Hence, we never know if we are acting consistently.*

The axioms of revealed preference have been part of the foundations of economics since they were formulated by Paul Samuelson in 1947. They have allowed economists to continue to use the calculus of utilitarianism even though utilitarianism had ceased to be a fashionable philosophical doctrine. Further, they enabled economists to give a particular and special meaning to the term rationality. In modern economics, rationality is equated with consistency.

But consistency, as Ralph Waldo Emerson said, is "the hobgoblin of little minds, adored by little statesmen and philosophers and divines." Ordinary people do not equate rationality with consistency. It is consistent to persist in the belief that there are fairies at the bottom of the garden, even if it is not rational.

Nor is it inconsistent to make different meal choices if one dines at the same restaurant on successive nights. Of course, it would be easy to reassert

J. Kay (✉)
St John's College, Oxford, UK

© Springer International Publishing AG 2017
B.S. Frey, D. Iselin (eds.), *Economic Ideas You Should Forget*,
DOI 10.1007/978-3-319-47458-8_35

consistency by insisting that the two situations are not in fact the same. The prior history has changed the circumstances of the meal choice, and, therefore, it could be claimed that the behavior is "rational." However, this saves the day only by removing the claim of rationality of any content. Whatever we do must be rational otherwise we wouldn't have done it. Thus, any behavior can be rescued from the charge of irrationality in this way.

The problem is that in a complex world, there are no objective means of defining whether two situations are in fact the same. This is particularly problematic when this axiomatic approach is applied to choices made with imperfect knowledge and under radical uncertainty, which in practice describes most choices we make in the real world.

However, the same cannot be said for choices we make in a psychologist's laboratory. Behavioral economics has long been used to berate us for our "irrationality." Much of what is described as "irrationality" is simply a manifestation of the coping strategies humans have developed over millennia to deal with complex situations of which they only have limited understanding or knowledge. In a laboratory, scientists then invite hapless subjects to make decisions in wholly artificial situations in which the problem is completely specified—at least to the satisfaction of the experimenter. When subjects read a legend that insists that "a bird in **the the** hand" is the same as "a bird in **the** hand," it is the designer of the experiment, not the subject, who is making the mistake.

Perhaps we would do better to adopt the Oxford English Dictionary's definition of rationality: "endowed with reason, exercising one's reason in a proper manner, having sound judgment."

# There Ain't No Such Thing as a Free Lunch: The Myth of Expansionary Consolidations

## Gebhard Kirchgässner

When budget deficits become too large and public debt is increasing too fast, i. e., fiscal policy is no longer sustainable, fiscal consolidations become necessary. Public expenditure has to be reduced and/or taxes have to be raised. According to estimates of the International Monetary Fund (IMF), a 1 % of GDP fiscal consolidation reduces—on average—real GDP by about 0.5 % and raises the unemployment rate by about 0.3 % points. Thus, a major fiscal consolidation can lead to social problems, sometimes even to severe social unrest. The hope is, of course, that such a policy leads in the long run to a more sustainable fiscal policy accompanied by an economic upswing that helps to solve the social problems.

In their 2010 paper, Alesina and Ardagna presented a different view which goes back to considerations of Giavazzi and Marco in 1990. If private economic agents realise the budget cut and believe that the new, sustainable fiscal policy will continue, they might react by immediately increasing investment and/or consumption. Thus, in contrast to traditional wisdom, a fiscal contraction might be accompanied by an economic upswing or at least not by an economic contraction. They presented some examples for such a situation. This argument played a major role in the discussion about how EU member countries should behave during the European debt crisis; it supported the request for austerity policy.

G. Kirchgässner (✉)
Universität St. Gallen, SIAW-HSG, Bodanstrasse 8, 9000 St. Gallen, Switzerland
e-mail: Gebhard.Kirchgaessner@unisg.ch

© Springer International Publishing AG 2017
B.S. Frey, D. Iselin (eds.), *Economic Ideas You Should Forget*,
DOI 10.1007/978-3-319-47458-8_36

A critical discussion of this paper showed that none of the examples was convincing; either the fiscal consolidation was not in an economic downswing or there were other factors as, for example, a strong devaluation which might have prevented a further downswing. The IMF and others, acknowledging the theoretical possibility of such a development, stated that there was no chance for such an effect in the current situation in Europe. Given the low interest rates, it cannot be accompanied by expansionary monetary policy. Moreover, if many countries undertake fiscal consolidations, the negative effect on GDP is magnified. In taking up the IMF's arguments, the Economist concludes: "Most people believe that fiscal consolidations are helpful in the long run. Expecting them to be painless looks like wishful thinking."

Economics is often called a "dismal science". The reason for this is that economists typically tell the people that everything has its costs and benefits: "There ain't no such thing as a free lunch." That two economists propagate fiscal consolidations as a possibility for such a free lunch is at any rate astonishing.

There is, moreover, another aspect that is politically highly relevant. Fiscal consolidations are sometimes necessary but nevertheless painful. In many cases, poor people suffer the most. Take, for example, Greece. Between 2008 and 2013, unemployment rose from 7.8 to 27.5 %. An economist demanding a fiscal consolidation has to explain why he thinks that the sacrifice of the poor is unavoidable and, by this way, justified. To promise citizens something that will not happen does not only impair the reputation of the economists' profession but also the trust in our economic system. Thus, let us forget the idea of expansionary consolidations!

# Government Hurts the Economy More Than It Helps

Margaret Levi

>> *Without a state, there is no economy, no society, and not even a Silicon Valley. So forget about the illusion that the government is just an obstacle to economic growth.*

To quote Nobel Laureate Douglass North (1981, p. 2), "The existence of the state is essential for economic growth; the state, however, is the source of man-made economic decline." Long debunked but still kicking is this knee-jerk view, held by too many contemporary economists, that only the second half of this proposition is true and, moreover, that it is true at all times and in all places. Adam Smith, long considered the progenitor of theories of the limited state, was actually one of the first modern advocates of productive government involvement in the economy. For Smith, it is private interest embodied in good husbandry governed by the protection of property rights that produces public virtue. He advocated a combination of the division of labor, the invisible hand, and—lest it be forgotten—appropriate public laws, policies, and practices that enable individuals with wide-ranging capacities to generate economic growth for the country in which they reside.

States can harm the economy and, equally important, society; when governments do more harm than good is a contextual question. There are plenty

M. Levi (✉)
Stanford University, Stanford, CA, USA

© Springer International Publishing AG 2017
B.S. Frey, D. Iselin (eds.), *Economic Ideas You Should Forget*,
DOI 10.1007/978-3-319-47458-8_37

of examples where states have overreached or protected the interests of an elite, an often economically or technologically reactionary elite. In such instances (and others), the state ". . .is the source of man-made economic decline."

But without a state, there is no economy or society. That is indisputable. And it is not simply the laws protecting property rights that do the positive work here. It is also regulations that restrict property rights in order to protect the public from injurious pharmaceuticals, workplace practices, or poor drivers, just to name a few. It is not only the establishment of a system of justice and national defense but also a court system that adjudicates disputes and a legislature that determines when war is appropriate. Smith recognized the importance of government provision of infrastructure, especially when it was in no actor's private interest to supply a public good. William Gates, Jr., Warren Buffet, and other extraordinarily successful capitalists make the even stronger claim that government provision of major infrastructure—physical and human—allows capitalism to thrive and the American dream to become possible. Silicon Valley could not have existed without government subsidies, and the advanced research that innovations in technology and science depend upon requires public investment. So do roads, train stations, ports, and airports.

The history of the world is the history of technological and demographic change, and successful economies require adaptable work forces. Education, social insurance, and retraining are necessary government programs—although their forms and extents can and will vary. And all of these come with a price tag. Resistance to paying for what we need does not mean we should not tax and spend, as the proponents of austerity seem to believe. Rather, it is the cost that we as a society must bear to make the economy stronger.

The bottom line is that public actions undergird private success and make, in the words of Douglass North, "the existence of the state [. . .] essential for economic growth." Full stop.

# The Motivated Armchair Approach to Preferences

## Siegwart Lindenberg

>> *Let's forget about the economic idea that a person's preferences are complete and follow a transitive ordering.*

Big strides have been made in the research of social preferences. But economists should drop both the idea that a person's preferences represent a complete and transitive ordering and that conflicting preferences must belong to two different types of people. The really interesting question then is: if this is wrong, what is right?

The upshot of this piece is that a motivated armchair approach to preferences that prioritizes tractability in model building over realism is a serious obstacle to progress in microeconomics. Such an approach makes economists miss out on paying attention to the most important source of adaptation and flexibility in daily life. The first speed of adaptation (genetic encoding) is very slow, and the second speed (phenotypic plasticity, i.e., learning) is much faster but still very slow with regard to changing situations, but it is the third speed of shifting the salience of mindsets (i.e., overarching goals) that provides the adaptability and dynamics of behavior in day-to-day interactions. Mindsets only influence behavior to the degree that they are salient (i.e., activated). Like shadows, sets of preferences are activated along with the activation of mindsets.

S. Lindenberg (✉)
University of Groningen and Tilburg University, Groningen, The Netherlands

B.S. Frey, D. Iselin (eds.), *Economic Ideas You Should Forget*,
DOI 10.1007/978-3-319-47458-8_38

**89**

There are three major mindsets: (1) the gain mindset, directed at increasing one's resources, such as money; (2) the hedonic mindset, directed at feeling good; and (3) the normative mindset, directed at behaving appropriately. That it is just these three makes great evolutionary sense. At any given moment, all three mindsets are activated to some degree (thus, there are always multiple motives), but one will be the most salient and largely determine what we pay attention to and what we ignore, what parts of our knowledge system are activated, what we expect others to do, which goal criteria are important, and, importantly, which set(s) of preferences are activated.

By now, we know much about the workings of mindsets and thus about the situational activation of mindsets (together with the respective set of preferences). Any situation that clearly signals that one is part of a joint effort (converging interests and common goals) or that one contributes to a meaningful collective result will increase the salience of the normative mindset, as will the observed respect for norms by others and legitimate sanctions. Observed disrespect for norms, cues of social distance, and illegitimate sanctions will have the opposite effect. The gain mindset will reliably increase in salience when the costs of behavior increase, when situations turn competitive, and, more generally, when costs and benefits are expressed in terms of a medium of exchange (such as money). The hedonic mindset reliably increases in salience when cues in the situation create or activate threats or affordances for the satisfaction of fundamental needs (such as hunger, sex, comfort, status, or affection), frustrate expectations, or create anxiety. The mechanisms that govern the shifting salience of mindsets also explain which factors stabilize mindsets (and thus preferences) across different situations: values and identities. But these stabilizers do not lead to fixed preference types because they can be and often are overruled by situational factors. In short, by now, we know much about the workings of preferences, and we know how important the third speed of adaptation is, so that there is no reasonable defense left for prioritizing the tractability of model building beyond dealing with the dynamics of shifting saliences.

# Economics Is Based on Scientific Methods

## Michael McAleer

>> *Economics is a social science, but it is not based on the scientific method.*

Economics is a social science that describes the factors that determine the optimal allocation of resources subject to the budget constraints of individuals in society. The discipline uses models to capture the relationships among variables for purposes of analysis and forecasting. A theory is intended to provide rational explanations for observable and/or latent, that is, non-observable, data. Theories are typically explained through the use of models. A model is a set of assumptions, and such assumptions may be based on axioms or hypotheses. Economists can and do disagree on which assumptions might be classified as axioms or which are hypotheses.

Axioms are propositions that are regarded as self-evident, true, and, therefore, are not tested. A well-known example is the purported rationality of individuals, which is widely regarded as an axiom, although it has been tested in experimental economics. Hypotheses are propositions that are not regarded as self-evidently true and, hence, are tested. A null hypothesis is the assumption to be tested, while an alternative hypothesis is typically used to provide the power of the test, that is, the probability of rejecting a false null hypothesis

M. McAleer (✉)
Department of Quantitative Finance, National Tsing Hua University, Hsinchu, Taiwan

© Springer International Publishing AG 2017                      **91**
B.S. Frey, D. Iselin (eds.), *Economic Ideas You Should Forget*,
DOI 10.1007/978-3-319-47458-8_39

using empirical evidence based on real data. Null hypotheses can be rejected using statistical tests and/or appropriate prediction/forecasting criteria. Predictions or forecasts arising from models are statements or inferences regarding unknown events. Simple correlations capture linear relationships between two variables, while information criteria, such as R-squared, describe multiple correlations. Correlations should not be confused with causality, which is based on the concept of cause and effect, where one event precedes another, and the former is interpreted to be at least partially responsible for the latter.

The scientific method investigates, specifies, tests, and does or does not reject statistical hypotheses based on measurable empirical or latent information, corrects existing knowledge as encapsulated in theories, and forms a basis for acquiring new knowledge and developing new theories. The scientific process is essentially a modelling cycle, whereby existing theories are specified as models to be tested using empirical evidence, which might be based on real, experimental, or simulated data. Theories that are rejected on the basis of empirical evidence should be discarded and subsequently replaced with theories that have not yet been rejected by the weight of empirical evidence.

Apart from statistical hypothesis tests, the only so-called statistical test of causality in economics is the Granger causality test, which is effectively a time series test of predictability rather than causality. Most predictions in economics are based on models that may appear to have reasonably accurate forecasting properties, but which might or might not have been rejected using statistical hypothesis tests. Rejecting a null hypothesis should not be confused with rejecting a theory because axioms, which form part of a theoretical framework, are not rejected since they are not tested. Although correlations and forecasts are taken seriously, hypothesis testing is not important in economics as no economic theory has ever been rejected based on statistical hypothesis testing. To state the obvious, economics is a social science, but the discipline is not based on the scientific method.

# The Death of Distance

## Peter Nijkamp

**》** *The world is flat and geographic distance does not matter anymore. Wrong, physical distance friction costs may decline as a result of information and communication technology, but there are still many other distance frictions that cause economic actors to cluster in space.*

For centuries, distance was the economist's anchor point for analyzing spatial-economic interactions in the form of transport, trade, migration, commuting, or tourism. The central role of distance in economic research originates from the economic costs of bridging geographic distances. This "truth" is clearly incorporated in all gravity models in economics, which are essentially inspired by Newtonian physics. The new economic geography (NEG) introduced by Paul Krugman and others takes the cost friction of distance as a cornerstone for analyzing economic interdependencies in space.

Recently, several propositions have been voiced, which argue that in a modern economy, the role of information and communication technology (ICT)—and in particular digital technology—is so pervasive that geographic distance no longer matters. This claim of *the death of distance* has led to a new economic paradigm characterized by the proposition that *the world is flat.*

P. Nijkamp (✉)
Tinbergen Institute, Amsterdam, Netherlands

© Springer International Publishing AG 2017
B.S. Frey, D. Iselin (eds.), *Economic Ideas You Should Forget,*
DOI 10.1007/978-3-319-47458-8_40

Consequently, geography would no longer count in the modern space economy: competition is everywhere and is not determined by geographic locations, provided of course that they have open access to ubiquitous open cyberspace. This phenomenon would have great impacts on the dispersion of economic activity on our planet: the landscape of our world would become more uniform and flatter.

The *death of distance* hypothesis—and the related *flat world* hypothesis—does not seem to be very credible for several reasons. First, it is not true that Internet access—or, more generally, access to cyberspace—is uniformly distributed across the world. There are millions of people that have never even made a simple telephone call! Consequently, our world has been—and still is—rather spiky. Second, the access to digital technology is not identical to the use of this technology. Thus, demand conditions are critical for the benefits that accrue from the use of ICT and open cyberspace. Third, the advantages of Internet use in densely populated areas—through a varied portfolio of agglomeration advantages of all kinds—are much higher than in isolated areas. Distance friction is more than costly physical separation but finds its counterpart in locational benefits. Fourth, the combination of physical clusters and urbanization advantages and of virtual Internet advantages provides a strong competitive position to urban areas, with the necessary effect that large cities will nowadays tend to grow and lead even to a more spiky spatial-economic landscape. And finally, even if physical distance friction costs decline as a result of ICT, there are still many other distance frictions that cause economic actors to cluster in space. This is clearly reflected in the French "proximity school" where proximity—as the reverse of physical distance—is seen as a major organizing cluster paradigm for the spatial-economic landscapes of our world. Proximity is interpreted here as a connectivity principle bringing economic agents together from a social, cognitive, entrepreneurial, technological, or cultural perspective.

In conclusion, the current trend toward massive urbanization all over the world is a structural undercurrent of a modern and technologically advanced global economy, in which the idea of *the death of distance* and of a *flat world* is the least plausible assumption. A "flying carpet" world is a myth in economics.

# Dump the Concept of Rationality Into the Deep Ocean

## Karl-Dieter Opp

>> *Let's dump the concept of rationality. Already the definition of "rationality" is unclear.*

I am professor of sociology who studied economics, and I am an advocate of the rational choice approach in sociology that applies the economic model of man to the explanation of phenomena that sociologists are interested in. Thus, I feel competent in dealing with the concept of rationality.

One might assume that a concept so pervasive not only in economics but in political science and philosophy as well is defined in a clear and consistent way. However, this is definitely not the case. A vast number of authors write about "rationality" without outlining what they mean. To be sure, many authors define the concept, but one finds dozens of meanings such as:

1. Rational = a person's preferences are consistent (transitive, complete).
2. Rational = a person maximizes his or her objective utility ("objective" means "from the perspective of an observer").
3. Rational = a person maximizes his or her subjective utility ("subjective" means "from the person's perspective").

K.-D. Opp (✉)
University of Leipzig, Leipzig, Germany

University of Washington, Seattle, WA, USA

© Springer International Publishing AG 2017
B.S. Frey, D. Iselin (eds.), *Economic Ideas You Should Forget*,
DOI 10.1007/978-3-319-47458-8_41

4. Rational = a person deliberates before he or she acts.
5. Rational = a person is fully informed about the consequences of his or her behavior.

Which definition is appropriate then? Remember a basic fact of formal logic: a definition is a mere convention about how to use a concept. The previous examples are thus suggestions how to use the word "rational." Such definitions do not say anything about the *actual usage* of a concept in everyday life. If authors wish to capture *actual usage*, they need empirical research. A definition does not capture the *essence* of a phenomenon either—whatever "essence" means. Because a (nominal) definition is not true or false, the criterion for accepting it is its *usefulness*. The question then is what the criteria are to judge the usefulness of a definition.

To what extent is one of those five definitions of "rational" useful? We do not know. I have never found an author who gives a detailed account of why he or she introduces a certain definition and not another one.

A definition is useful, among other things, if it is a *shortcut* for a long sentence and, thus, saves time and space. In the five frequently found definitions, the word "rational" is a shortcut for the expression to the right. In this particular case, using "rational" as the shortcut has also a disadvantage: the term has several nonscientific meanings, so the reader often associates other meanings than those stipulated in the definition. The question is then whether the gain of a shortcut is so high that taking into account possible misunderstandings is worthwhile.

To illustrate, why do we need the first definition of rational? We could simply speak of consistency—a term that needs definition as well and thus there is no gain in the abbreviation. The same holds for the second and third definition of rational: why not simply speak of objective or subjective utility maximization? And lastly, we don't need the fourth or fifth definition either: one could simply speak of deliberation or "full information," respectively, so that, again, there is no gain of the definition.

These examples suggest that using "rational" or "rationality" is not at all useful. It is even detrimental: the benefits of saving time or space are minimal and the costs are possible misunderstandings. Thus, forget about the concept of rationality. Try to avoid it—you'll be surprised how easy this is.

# Pay for Performance Raises Performance

Margit Osterloh

» *Variable pay for performance raises performance. A very efficient idea, but a wrong one. Fixed salaries supplemented by awards and feedback are much more efficient in improving performance.*

Pay for performance intends to raise performance by paying bonuses when certain targets are reached. However, for complex and ambiguous tasks, evidence-based studies have been unable to show that this is the case. The widespread implementation of pay for performance in areas like management, research, healthcare, or public service, therefore, is not justified. In contrast, variable pay for performance worsens performance of such tasks. Nonetheless, enthusiasm for pay for performance remains strong.

Proponents of variable pay for performance refer to standard economics, in particular to the principal agent view. This theory builds on the model of the self-interested *homo economicus*. It accepts–as a matter of course–that

M. Osterloh (✉)
University of Zurich, Zurich, Switzerland

University of Basel, Basel, Switzerland

CREMA – Center for Research in Economics, Management and the Arts, Zurich, Switzerland

© Springer International Publishing AG 2017                                    **97**
B.S. Frey, D. Iselin (eds.), *Economic Ideas You Should Forget*,
DOI 10.1007/978-3-319-47458-8_42

compensation should provide big rewards for outstanding and penalties for poor performance.

However, the idea of enhancing performance by pay for performance is wrong in itself. This criticism is substantiated by psychological or behavioral economics and motivation psychology. Many field and laboratory experiments show that people to a considerable extent have pro-social preferences. They work not only in order to earn as much money as possible but also enjoy their work. They are motivated intrinsically and not only extrinsically.

There are five counterproductive effects of variable pay for performance:

1. *Multitasking effect.* Variable pay for performance leads to a goal displacement of extrinsically motivated people. They concentrate on easy-to-measure tasks, which are therefore easy to be rewarded. Tasks which are not easy to measure (e.g., sustainable performance, long-term health, or organizational citizenship behavior) are ignored. With complex and ambiguous tasks, pay for performance is motivating the wrong kinds of behavior.
2. *Self-serving bias.* Empirical evidence shows that most people suffer from an unconscious self-serving bias. Particularly in ambiguous environments, they tend to interpret situations in a way that is advantageous to them. This bias cannot be lessened by penalties, because it is not consciously controlled. Examples are auditors that approve questionable accounts, moneylenders who sell mortgages to people who should not buy houses, or physicians that undertake unnecessary medical treatments.
3. *Gaming the system.* There exists a lot of empirical evidence to confirm that pay for performance promotes manipulative behavior of CEOs, athletes, and other people. Examples are "cooking the books" or doping. As a consequence, pay for performance does not reward performance but rewards manipulation.
4. *Self-selection-effect.* Variable pay for performance attracts extrinsically motivated persons more than intrinsically motivated individuals and thus reinforces the necessity for external control measures.
5. *Crowding out effect.* If intrinsically motivated persons are induced to act according to external control, their intrinsic motivation is reduced. They enjoy their work less and feel less obliged to follow pro-social norms because their autonomy is curtailed. If the reduced intrinsic motivation is not compensated for by external incentives, performance decreases and a vicious circle sets in.

As a consequence, with jobs characterized by high complexity and ambiguity, variable pay for performance should be avoided. Instead, fixed salaries supplemented by awards and feedback are much more efficient to improve performance.

# Home Ownership Is Good

## Andrew J. Oswald

>> *Everybody should have their own home. Bad idea. High home ownership is linked to high unemployment.*

"The dream of a property-owning democracy is alive, and we will help you fulfil it," Mr David Cameron, former Prime Minister of the UK, speech given in August 2015

It is widely believed that a sign of national success is that a large number of citizens own their own homes (i.e. are 'owner occupiers'). This view is wrong.

Home ownership impairs the vitality of the labor market and, in the jargon of Milton Friedman, slowly grinds out greater rates of joblessness. The tax breaks given to home ownership in most western nations (Switzerland is one of the few exceptions) are also hugely expensive for tax payers and divert resources away from genuinely entrepreneurial activities. Thus, despite what presidents and prime ministers think, the world would be a better place if nearly everyone rented their homes.

The home ownership elasticity of unemployment appears, according to existing research, to be close to unity. High levels of home ownership do not destroy jobs in the current year; they tend to do so years later (as I showed in a 2013 NBER Working Paper with David G. Blanchflower). Unless these long

A.J. Oswald (✉)
University of Warwick, Coventry, UK

© Springer International Publishing AG 2017                    **99**
B.S. Frey, D. Iselin (eds.), *Economic Ideas You Should Forget*,
DOI 10.1007/978-3-319-47458-8_43

linkages are understood, the deleterious consequences of high levels of home ownership cannot be appreciated.

What mechanisms are at work? The most compelling evidence comes from the United States. High home ownership in a given US state is associated with:

(1) Lower labor mobility
(2) Longer commutes
(3) Fewer new firms and establishments (through the power of zoning laws supported by home owners)

It should be emphasized that this is after statistical controls for a wide range of possible confounding factors. Consistent results have emerged from a European study by Laamanen from the University of Tampere (2013).

Home owners are not more unemployed than renters, and that is the wrong way to think about the problem. Instead, the housing market generates important negative externalities for the labor market. High home ownership is a major reason for the high unemployment rates of the European nations in the post-war era. Home ownership is bad not good.

# Coase Theorem

## Eric A. Posner

**»** *Forget about the Coase Theorem. It determines the status quo and hinders better designed taxes.*

The Coase Theorem states that if transaction costs are zero, the efficient allocation of resources will occur, regardless of the initial distribution of entitlements, so long as the entitlements are well defined. Many scholars have cited the Coase Theorem as support for various claims—that government regulation is of limited importance, that Pigouvian taxes are ill-advised, and that government should focus on ensuring that property rights are well defined. However, the Coase Theorem does not support these claims or have any useful empirical or normative implications.

One puzzle about the Coase Theorem is what is meant by "transaction costs." A possible interpretation is the physical and opportunity costs of negotiating and drafting a contract. But if this is what transaction costs mean, then the Coase Theorem tells us just that parties will not enter into certain low-value transactions because the benefits are less than the transaction costs. This is not an interesting or useful insight.

E.A. Posner (✉)
University of Chicago Law School, Chicago, IL, USA
e-mail: eric_posner@law.uchicago.edu

© Springer International Publishing AG 2017
B.S. Frey, D. Iselin (eds.), *Economic Ideas You Should Forget*,
DOI 10.1007/978-3-319-47458-8_44

A more common interpretation is that transaction costs mean asymmetries of information. If information costs are zero, parties will bargain to optimal distributions; otherwise, they will or might not.

But if this is the right interpretation, then when transaction costs are zero or low, there is also no need for a market, as Hayek argued. The government can determine efficient outcomes. And if information costs are high, then the Coase Theorem by its own terms has no implications.

Many scholars have claimed that the Coase Theorem implies a specific normative agenda. One is deregulation when transaction costs are low: if the government cannot affect the allocation of entitlements, it should not bother to try. However, there are hardly any cases where transaction costs are so low that government intervention is futile. Even when only two people interact, and both are sophisticated, information asymmetries can block the efficient outcome. The government faces an array of possible property-rights systems that minimize this risk to different degrees. It must choose and enforce the optimal system. An agenda of "deregulation" doesn't tell us which system is optimal.

Other scholars argue that the Coase Theorem indicates that the government can and should help reduce information costs, enabling parties to achieve efficient outcomes, and the government can do this by clearly defining and enforcing property rights. Pigouvian taxation and other forms of regulation are then unnecessary.

However, this argument, like the first, doesn't tell us what it means for the government to clearly define and enforce property rights. Traditional "simple" property rights give owners monopoly power, which interferes with bargaining as long as information is imperfect. The government produces better outcomes by allowing people to violate property rights as long as they pay damages than by enforcing property rights strictly. The damages are roughly the same as a Pigouvian tax—the target of Coase's critique.

Transaction costs can also be high when externalities harm a large number of agents. In such cases, enforcing property rights entrenches the status quo, blocking bargains to efficient outcomes. The Coase Theorem agrees that bargaining cannot solve this problem, but some scholars have taken the Theorem as a rebuke to Pigouvian taxes, which cannot account for the reciprocal nature of harm as well as bargaining can. Be that as it may, the Coase Theorem provides no guidance in such settings. It is an empirical question whether Pigouvian taxes improve over the status quo in many-agent settings; it may also be the case that better-designed taxes can do so.

While there is much of value in Coase's work, which helped stimulate interest in the optimal design of legal and market institutions, the Coase Theorem should be forgotten.

# Poverty Is Good for Development

## Martin Ravallion

**»** *The idea that poverty promotes economic development should be rejected. The arguments made for this idea are unconvincing. Theory and evidence suggest that poverty is more likely to limit development.*

There are two prominent versions of the idea that poverty promotes economic development. One version argues that poverty incentivizes workers, thus creating a strong, globally competitive economy. Another version postulates that higher marginal products of capital in poorer (capital-scarce) countries entail that they enjoy higher growth rates, such that they automatically catch up to rich countries in due course. Both versions should be rejected.

The first version can be traced back to the mercantilist thinking of the sixteenth through eighteenth centuries, which viewed the balance of trade (BoT) as indicative of the prosperity and power of the realm. A higher BoT was seen to require cheap raw materials (for which colonies proved useful) and cheap, and therefore poor, labor at home. Hunger was assumed to encourage work. Proponents of this idea were also opposed to direct income support for poor families, arguing that it discouraged work and would increase the wages demanded.

M. Ravallion (✉)
Department of Economics, Georgetown University, Washington, DC, USA

© Springer International Publishing AG 2017
B.S. Frey, D. Iselin (eds.), *Economic Ideas You Should Forget*,
DOI 10.1007/978-3-319-47458-8_45

Mercantilism regularly resurfaces in political debates across the globe (including in the 2016 Presidential race in the USA). But it has been rejected by most economists. Famously, in his *Inquiry into the Nature and Causes of the Wealth of Nations*, Adam Smith argued for a broader conception of development, based on command over commodities. Over the subsequent 100 years or so, Smith's insights opened the way to eventually ushering in progress against poverty as a goal for development, rather than a threat to it. Similarly, Smith saw higher real wages as desirable and favored antipoverty policies, such as subsidies to support the schooling of children from poor families.

The second version has more recent origins, namely in the higher growth rates seen in the developing world in the new millennium. It is what Wolf, Mahbubani, and others dub "The Great Convergence," whereby poor countries eventually catch up to rich ones in the future global economy.

Yet, while the recent economic success of China and India is undeniable, the idea that poorer countries tend *as a rule* to grow faster finds little or no support in the data. Rather, the modern literature on growth empirics suggests that there is convergence conditional on the various determinants of long-run income, such as education, health, and efficiency-promoting policy reforms (see *Economic Growth* by Barro and Sala-i-Martin). Growth economists appreciate that this is best understood as a dynamic adjustment process, as economies with diminishing marginal products of capital, but different starting points move toward their respective steady-state ("long-run") equilibria. That is clearly quite different to saying that poor countries will catch up to rich ones.

Indeed, I have argued elsewhere that theory and evidence suggest instead that developing countries starting out with a higher poverty rate tend to have *lower* long-run incomes, controlling for their initial means and other observed determinants of long-run mean income (see my 2012 *American Economic Review* paper). This holds even though conditional convergence is also evident in the transitional dynamics. I have also found that countries with a higher initial poverty rate need a higher rate of growth to have the same proportionate impact on the incidence of poverty.

Again the bad idea is revealed to be just that. Poverty is best seen as an impediment to development rather than its precondition for it.

# Markets Are Efficient

Jean-Charles Rochet

>> *The Efficient Market Hypothesis (EMH) might not apply well to labor markets, but it works on money markets. Not true. Even money markets can be grossly inefficient.*

Assuming efficient markets in economics is a bit like neglecting air resistance in physics. It allows developing beautiful models and using powerful mathematical techniques, but the simple fact that there is air everywhere around us (otherwise, we could not live) or that actual markets exhibit all kinds of imperfections is not enough to discard such assumptions. All theories require simplifying assumptions, even if those seem very implausible. The real problem is: are the beautiful models developed with these assumptions of any use for understanding the real world?

Conventional wisdom is that the answer depends on what particular aspect of the real world we want to study. For example, if we study the free fall of a rock, neglecting air resistance is fine. If it is the free fall of a sheet of paper, omitting air resistance does not work at all. The same is true for the efficient market hypothesis (EMH): most economists would agree that it does not work well on labor markets, but few would criticize its application to money

J.-C. Rochet (✉)
University of Zurich, Zurich, Switzerland

© Springer International Publishing AG 2017

B.S. Frey, D. Iselin (eds.), *Economic Ideas You Should Forget*,

DOI 10.1007/978-3-319-47458-8_46

markets, i.e., the markets where banks and large corporations get short-term finance in different currencies.

Money markets are very liquid, transaction costs are small, and participants are smart professionals who understand what they are doing. Thus, they are a good candidate for the EMH, and one of its most important implications is the absence of arbitrage opportunities, i.e., the impossibility to make an assured profit without investing any funds.

Some economists view it as the only "universal law" in economics and as an extension of the law of one price. It is the basis for the powerful and elegant models of mathematical finance.

A standard technique of arbitrage between national money markets is carry trade: borrowing in one currency and lending in another, while hedging currency risk by using derivative instruments. This arbitrage is theoretically possible without any funds (one borrows in one currency the amount lent in the other) and without taking any risk (since the trade is hedged by a derivative contract).

Most mathematical finance courses use carry trade as a motivating example. It is easy to see, indeed, that if money markets are efficient, a simple relation must exist between interest rates in different currencies, called the covered interest parity formula. This is the most basic formula in mathematical finance.

Alas, even this basic formula does not hold. It was severely violated several times in the global financial crisis (GFC) of 2007–2009. Thus, even money markets can sometimes be grossly inefficient, as they can exhibit persistent, sizable, and seize-able arbitrage opportunities. The reason is that any arbitrage, even if it looks totally risk-free, needs capital to operate properly, and capital is scarce since the GFC.

Ultimately, there seems to be no "universal law" in economics. This should not be a reason to reject models. Rather, this is an encouragement to develop alternative models that may be less elegant and more accurate and take into account the frictions that matter significantly in actual markets.

# CEOs Are Paid for Talent

## Katja Rost

**》**CEO's exorbitant salaries can at least partly be explained by their talent. Sounds deserved, but it's not.

A few economists still believe that the extraordinary high and yearly increasing salaries for CEOs can at least be partially explained by talent. Underlying this are elaborate theories and models such as an increasing demand by a simultaneous shortage of talented people, which is driven by external factors like globalization, technological progress, demographic change, or a general shift from firm-specific to transferable skills. All these explanations share the assumption that marginal differences in talent get extraordinarily paid in the CEO market because of Zipf's law. Such superstar effects in salaries are driven by "imperfect substitution"—meaning that firms prefer to have the best CEO rather than the second and third best together—and by "scale" in production—implying that in international companies consisting of thousands of employees, one CEO can reach and manage a large and diverse work force.

The main problem of these models is that the micro-mechanisms underlying selection processes within organizations are neglected. It is assumed that selection processes obey the law of multistage tournaments with the top talents in one stage progressing to the next. Within organizations, "talent" or

K. Rost (✉)
University of Zurich, Zurich, Switzerland

© Springer International Publishing AG 2017
B.S. Frey, D. Iselin (eds.), *Economic Ideas You Should Forget*,
DOI 10.1007/978-3-319-47458-8_47

employee performance is not easily measured, especially not in management jobs, where tasks are complex and people work together in teams or projects to achieve a desired outcome. First, in such a context, "talent" is a multidimensional construct accounting for analytic or social skills. Each dimension is valuable, and it is not clear how to weigh these dimensions against each other. Second, many dimensions are hidden to the observer, for example, because they can only be obtained in the long run like radical innovation or by chance like the detection of sabotage or corruption. Third, performance evaluations in organizations are biased. Because of stereotypes or homophily, they systematically (dis)advantage the careers of specific groups. Difficulties in capturing employee performance increase as people climb the career ladder, since the job becomes more complex and team oriented and the difficulties are particularly high for the best 25 % of workers because, while most people agree on who is a low or medium performer, only few can agree on who is among the top 5 % or even top 1 % of performers.

It shows that selection processes within firms and, in particular, for top performers at high career levels are imperfect and biased. It does not produce a transitive pecking order. In addition, information cascades play a major role in promotion decisions: people observe the upward promotion of a person within a firm and then—despite possible contradictions in their own information signals—promote this person one level further. It is therefore a superstition to believe that superstar effects in CEO salaries can be explained by talent or "imperfect substitution." Further, the "scale" in production argument has to be questioned. While it is well documented that CEOs get paid according to firm size, it seems questionable whether management skills improve in groups with unlimited size. Tournaments work perfectly in small, local settings. There is a high chance that the biggest frog will be selected within a pond. They do however fail in large, complex, and global markets, and luck and conformity produce a pecking order. Winners are extraordinarily rewarded because thousands of people participated in the lottery explaining why CEO pay and social inequality has increased so much.

# The Efficiency-Equity Tradeoff

## Jeffrey D. Sachs

>> *What is efficient might be inequitable. And what is equitable or fair, might be inefficient. Not true. In smart societies, equity and efficiency can rise together.*

A cliché of introductory economics courses is the trade-off between efficiency and equity. A market economy, it is said, is efficient: national income is maximized as profit-maximizing businesses and utility-maximizing consumers meet in the marketplace. The resulting market equilibrium may, however, be inequitable (unfair), with an excessive gap in income between the rich and poor. Taxing the rich to give money to the poor can then raise equity (fairness) but at the cost of distorting market incentives (such as incentives for hard work) and thereby lowering national income. The proverbial pie is shared more equally but the pie is smaller.

Dr. Arthur Okun, a wonderful US policy economist of the 1960s and 1970s (who was exceedingly kind to me when I was a fledging economist), used the metaphor of a leaky bucket. The bucket can carry money from the rich to the poor, but it leaks and loses money along the way. Should we favor taxing the rich $100 if only $50 reaches the poor? How about $20? How about $5?

J.D. Sachs (✉)
Columbia University, New York, NY, USA

© Springer International Publishing AG 2017
B.S. Frey, D. Iselin (eds.), *Economic Ideas You Should Forget*,
DOI 10.1007/978-3-319-47458-8_48

Alas, this fable is more alluring than truly insightful. The story highlights the importance of considering incentives when designing tax-and-transfer programs, but it misses the key reality of modern inequality. The most important component of income today is human capital, and the most important source of income inequality is the inequality of human capital, especially education and job market skills. The poor suffer not only from a deprivation of consumption but also of lifetime investments in human capital.

The key transfers aimed at reducing inequality are, therefore, not transfers of income per se, but transfers of human capital investments. Equitable societies ensure, through public spending, that every person, especially every child, receives the investments in health, nutrition, and education needed to build lifetime skills and health for productive employment and earnings. Such investments in human capital of children have some of the highest returns available to a society, yet the poorest households in society lack the cash income or borrowing capacity to make such investments out of their own finances.

There is, in short, no leaky bucket for the most important transfers that a society can and should make: universal provision of quality health care, childcare, pre-kindergarten schooling, and high-quality education from primary school through vocational or tertiary education. The ultimate educational attainment should depend on each child's aptitude rather than family income. In that case, $100 taken from wealthy households can easily produce far more than $100 in discounted lifetime earnings for poor households, by enabling these households to raise their children to their full physiological, cognitive, and scholastic potential.

Smart societies, like those in Scandinavia, are committed to this approach and recognize that equity and efficiency can thereby rise together; unwise societies, like my own country, the United States, fall very short of this ideal. All countries have recently committed themselves, at least on paper, to providing universal health care and quality education as part of the new Sustainable Development Goals (SDG 3 for health and SDG 4 for education) to be achieved by 2030.

Moreover, there is another important reason to doubt the leaky bucket story. It's hard to see how a society, sharply divided between rich and poor, could come close to even rudimentary efficiency, much less the high standard of raising every child to its potential. Unequal societies tend to be places of low social trust, unstable politics, and corruption. The rich may shield their incomes from the poor by manipulating politics (viz. America's addiction to unregulated campaign financing by the rich and powerful) at the cost of social unrest and a higher cost of doing business. Society then suffers in two ways: lower national income caused by crime, instability, and corruption and a decrement of psychological well-being of both the rich and poor due to a rise in social tensions, a deterioration of governance, and a decline in social trust and mutual support.

# Deterministic Trend of Inequality

## Christoph A. Schaltegger

**»** *Larger than life theories in economics tend to over-rate economic and technological change and tend to neglect institutions and politics. Forget about these deterministic approaches.*

The development of inequality in a capitalist society has always been at the forefront of economic thinking. Classical economists focused on the factor distribution of income—Ricardo predicted an ever-increasing share of national income would accrue to landowners and Marx to capitalists. Both observed the trends of their times and predicted them to go on unrestricted. In his seminal empirical work, Kuznets discovered the inverse U-shape of inequality, a finding explained by the shift from rural to industrial societies. Whereas the economic benefits of this shift were reaped by some lucky few at first, it later spread more broadly to society as a whole. Most recently, based on newly compiled data, Piketty predicts an ever-increasing accumulation of wealth based on consistently high returns to capital. Common to all of these theories is that economic and technological progress in a capitalist society deterministically causes inequality to develop in a certain direction. It is the search for "general" (Marx) or "fundamental" (Piketty) laws of capitalism.

C.A. Schaltegger (✉)
University of Lucerne, Lucerne, Switzerland

© Springer International Publishing AG 2017
B.S. Frey, D. Iselin (eds.), *Economic Ideas You Should Forget*,
DOI 10.1007/978-3-319-47458-8_49

However, these predictions neglect the institutional and political framework. Bruno Frey in the 1990s already postulated that institutions matter systematically. Recently, Acemoglu and Robinson, as well as Stiglitz, emphasize the major influence of political institutions on the development of technology, skill premia, and factor prices, which ultimately determine inequality. Just think of the institutional framework in which politics operate: trade, monetary, fiscal, and competition policy, the patent system, regulation of product, financial and labor markets, labor unions, publicly provided education, health services, infrastructure, and public transport. The distribution of market income is, to a high degree, politically determined. Additionally, redistribution via taxation and social security systems ensure a more equalized distribution of disposable income. But these authors go a step further in declaring political institutions to be endogenous, meaning that political institutions will evolve and adapt to changes in inequality. In the nineteenth century many of today's institutions didn't exist, and substantial imbalances in the income and wealth distribution were able to build up. Institutions were subsequently invented to correct imbalances. Today's institutions constantly adapt to forces like technological progress, globalization, or demographic changes.

If we look at the data, we discover major country-specific differences in the development of inequality. Thus, political institutions seem to be, at the very least, relevant. Consider the case of Switzerland, for which, together with Christian Frey, we constructed a time series of inequality based on tax data since 1933 showing an extraordinarily stable distribution of income. We conclude from this that in a political framework based on living federalism and direct democracy, where checks and balances impede the concentration of power, ongoing economic development and technological progress seem unable to push the income distribution persistently out of balance. Further we conclude that, if inequality builds up somewhere, this is necessarily a very country-specific phenomenon implying some kind of breakdown of political institutions rather than a "general law of capitalism."

# Quantitative Easing

## Kurt Schiltknecht

>> *It's time to end Quantitative Easing (QE). Central banks neglect that an unprecedented, huge increase in liquidity makes it impossible to form clear expectations about the impact of monetary policy on the economy.*

Central Banks acted forcefully in 2008 to prevent a financial crisis. As a result, the balance sheet of many central banks more than doubled. Such an increase does not create a problem as long as the liquidity is reduced in due time. However, this did not happen in the years after 2008, because the leading central banks were afraid of deflation. To counteract this threat, they injected even more liquidity. With interest rates close to 0 %, they could not increase liquidity by lowering the official rates further. Instead many central banks switched to "quantitative easing" (QE). They replaced the interest rate target by a target for the amount of bonds and other assets they intended to buy.

Despite the increase in liquidity in unprecedented amounts, GDP growth remained sluggish. This does not come as a surprise, because markets considered the increase to be temporary. The assumption that the increase in liquidity would be temporary resulted in very little growth and stable inflationary expectations. Central banks therefore tried to convince markets, with

K. Schiltknecht (✉)
Zurich, Switzerland

© Springer International Publishing AG 2017
B.S. Frey, D. Iselin (eds.), *Economic Ideas You Should Forget*,
DOI 10.1007/978-3-319-47458-8_50

explicit forward guidance, that the increases were going to be long-lasting. As a result long-term interest rates decreased a bit more. However, the recovery stayed subdued. When the former Chairman of the Federal Reserve, Ben Bernanke, was asked how confident he was that the theory of quantitative easing would work, he concluded: "The problem with QE is it works in practice but it doesn't work in theory." If an observation without theory is enough to justify an operation like QE, then governments could subsidize storks to solve the demographic problems in Europe.

Central banks are not questioning enough whether the introduction of QE and the small increases in growth were coincidental or why the upswing is only moderate in comparison to former cycles. Central banks are focusing too much on interest rates and the conventional monetary policy channels in financial markets. They neglect that an unprecedented, huge increase in liquidity makes it impossible to form clear expectations about the impact of monetary policy on the economy. Over the past 50 years I never encountered so many people being so uncertain about the future. Most people have big doubts that central banks can prevent inflation. They are wondering about the impact of a sharp reduction in liquidity on stock and housing prices, on exchange and interest rates, and the financing of the over-indebted countries. It is also an open question how central banks can get rid of the huge amount of public and private bonds in their balance sheets without disturbing financial markets. There is no doubt that the continuous expansion of the QE program has massively increased these uncertainties.

Growing uncertainties are poison for the economy and are offsetting the benefits of slightly lower interest rates. As long as monetary policy is fueling the uncertainty, markets will be unable to form reliable expectations. In such an environment, lower interest rates will stimulate neither borrowing nor consumption or investment. As a result banks will continue to sit on a huge amount of idle liquidity. The only beneficiaries of QE are speculators and short-term traders. It is wrong of proponents of QE to attribute the increase in GDP to QE. The improvement has much more to do with the wealth effect of lower oil and raw material prices.

A necessary condition for returning to a sustainable growth is a stable monetary environment. The best way to achieve it is to forget QE as a monetary tool and to return to medium-term targets for money and credit which have proven to be successful in the past.

# Hosting the Olympic Games

Sascha L. Schmidt

>> *Hosting the Olympics is not an economic boon, but may prove to be a societal one—increasing national happiness and thereby justifying enormously over-run budgets. Rethinking the traditional allocating method may further increase the happiness that hosting the Games produces.*

While athletes may still be cooling down from the recent Summer Olympic Games in Rio, economists remain at a boiling point when it comes to research on the Olympics. They have created bookshelves worth of publications about the economic effects of hosting the Games. So, what did they find? First and foremost cost overruns. Between 1960 and 2012, the Olympic Games consistently overran budgets, on average by 179 % in real and by 324 % in nominal terms as researchers from the University of Oxford found out. Although politicians and interest groups continually justify the overarching costs by promising future economic benefits, economists have a hard time finding any economic impact from hosting the Olympics, when engaging in ex post analysis of economic indicators like GDP, employment rate, and trade volume or via ex ante analysis of capital market expectations.

S.L. Schmidt (✉)
WHU – Otto Beisheim School of Management, Düsseldorf, Germany

© Springer International Publishing AG 2017                    **119**
B.S. Frey, D. Iselin (eds.), *Economic Ideas You Should Forget*,
DOI 10.1007/978-3-319-47458-8_51

Recent award decisions made by the International *Olympic Committee* have made economists painfully aware that their research on hosting the Olympics has minor or no effects on the real world. In particular, autocratic country leaders seem to be fine with hosting the Games even if they do not create economic gains and merely result in political benefits for themselves. The World Bank's Christopher Colford compares this to the declining Roman Empire, where the population was pacified with *panem et circenses* to obfuscate fundamental societal problems. However, is it amoral when leaders use the Olympics to make their subordinates happy rather than rich? What happens if people are more likely to expect happiness from the Olympics, rather than economic benefits?

Our recent study with representative survey data from 12,000 respondents in the USA and eleven European countries provides evidence that in regard to hosting the Olympics, people indeed care less about economic factors which bring them wealth than they do about social factors that make them happy—at least if you look at a national level. The reason is that the social welfare of people goes beyond classical economic data, actually including various intangible factors. Leading economists, like Ed Diener and Bruno Frey, have therefore long argued that happiness, as a proxy of social welfare, is what really matters for economic evaluation.

Thus, going forward, it may prove fruitful to devote more time and attention to the effect of hosting the Olympics on transnational happiness. Developing measures of actual and expected happiness gains from the Olympics, economic research could become a catalyst for out-of-the-box reform ideas that could revolutionize the hosting of the Games. This does not mean that economic facts no longer play a role, but that during times of chronic budget overruns, measures of expected happiness gains could play a decisive role when choosing the country and city to host the Olympic Games. The respective stakeholders can then decide whether spending the money for the forecasted happiness gain of the Olympics would be preferable to alternate targets of public spending (e.g., education, public health, or the art and cultural purposes). As long as higher overall happiness can be achieved, ideas such as hosting the Olympics multiple times in the same place, splitting the hosting across disciplines across multiple countries, or using a random drawing mechanism to award the Games to a host remain viable. Thinking beyond the traditional boundaries of economics and teaming up with researchers from other fields would enable economic research on the Olympics to evoke a greater impact among decision makers and help to keep the Olympic dream alive—within academia and for millions of people worldwide.

# Abolishing Cash as Solution Against the Evil

## Friedrich Schneider

**»** *Abolishing cash is hailed as an effective and simple solutions against many evils in the world, such as organized crimes or the shadow economy. Forget about that.*

Over the last 6 months intensive discussion has arisen about the abolition of cash. All of a sudden the abolition of cash could do miracles: If cash did not exist, there would be much less crime and the shadow economy would be greatly reduced, because all transactions undertaken in the shadow economy are generally made in cash. Could it really be that simple? Honestly, I think the idea that with the abolition of cash, organized crime, the financing of terrorism, and the shadow economy would be severely reduced or even disappear is irrational. In the following, I will elaborate on why I think it is a foolish idea, which should soon be forgotten.

F. Schneider (✉)
Johannes Kepler University of Linz, Linz, Austria

© Springer International Publishing AG 2017                           **121**
B.S. Frey, D. Iselin (eds.), *Economic Ideas You Should Forget*,
DOI 10.1007/978-3-319-47458-8_52

# What Are the Sources/Origins of Organized Crime?

Organized crime has been around for a long time because the profits from such crime are very high. Drug dealing has a global turnover of at least USD500 billion per year, and the net profit of drug dealing is at least USD350–400 billion per year. As drugs are illegal and heavily sanctioned in most countries, they can only be offered through criminal organizations, which are sure to earn high profits. On average the profit increases tenfold from the producer to the gross dealer and another tenfold from the gross dealer to the street. To reduce organized crime, for example, in the drug business, a (partial) legalization of drugs would be much more efficient and could wipe out all organized crime related to drugs. To reduce organized crime, one has to fight the reasons it occurs. Abolishing cash would by no means abolish drug or human trafficking.

# No Cash, No Shadow Economy?

Shadow economy activities in highly developed OECD countries are mostly undertaken because, first, the burden of taxes and social security contributions on labor is too high. Second, the regulation of craft and service activities is very intensive, adding another substantial cost factor. Hourly wages in the shadow economy are on average between 10 and 20 euros, while an official craftsman or service will cost between 80 and 100 euros per hour. If there were no cash, the transaction costs of shadow economy activities would rise, but the tremendous cost difference between an hour worked in the shadow economy and an hour of official labor would be only marginally reduced. Hence, by no means would the abolition of cash lead to a severe reduction in the shadow economy. Estimates suggest that shadow economy activities might be reduced by 3–5 %. For Germany, where the shadow economy is estimated at 320 billion euros, the reduction would only amount to 5–6 billion euros.

# Abolition of Cash: A Free Lunch?

If cash were to be entirely abolished, this would also lead to two severe disadvantages for a society. The **first** disadvantage concerns the fact, that, for example, I, as an Austrian member of the European Union, can decide how I want to spend my cash, no one controls it, and it is my free will to use my cash as I see fit. This is an elementary part of my freedom, and if cash were abolished, supervision by state authorities or big firms would be almost perfect. They could see what and when I buy and surveillance of people would assuredly be near perfect. A **second** disadvantage would be during severe blackouts; without cash, the whole economic system would break down. At least with cash a rudimentary economic life would still continue. Cash could be handed out by banks and I could still buy the necessities of life.

These two disadvantages of the abolition of cash are generally not discussed, and the possibility of cybercrime rises tremendously in cash-less societies. Of course, I am aware of the costs of cash, but they are still much lower than the advantages cash brings, as one of the oldest and most efficient forms of payment. Hence, abolishing cash is a crazy idea, which should not be considered further.

# Receiving Money and Not Having to Work Raises Happiness

Ronnie Schöb

**»** *The psychological consequences of unemployment lower well-being much more than the pecuniary burden of unemployment.*

The standard economic textbook is very clear about how to alleviate the burden of involuntary unemployment. If one fully compensates people who become unemployed for the associated income loss, they will not suffer from unemployment at all. In fact, they will become strictly better off. Full income compensation guarantees the same consumption opportunities as before job loss and staying jobless allows the unemployed to enjoy more leisure: receiving more money but not having to work thus raises their well-being.

Research on life satisfaction has challenged this traditional economic reasoning. When asked whether 'all things considered, how satisfied are you with your life as a whole these days?', unemployed people, on average, report substantially lower life satisfaction than employed people. The differences in reported life satisfaction remain substantial even after controlling for the income loss. But if it is not material hardship, what else makes unemployment so harmful?

Earlier studies on the misery of the unemployed hint at the losses of social contacts and time structure that a working day provides and at the forced

R. Schöb (✉)
Freie Universität Berlin, Berlin, Germany

© Springer International Publishing AG 2017
B.S. Frey, D. Iselin (eds.), *Economic Ideas You Should Forget*,
DOI 10.1007/978-3-319-47458-8_53

inactivity. Recent large-scale empirical studies do not confirm these hypotheses. In fact, it seems that unemployed people can restore their emotional balance by substituting more enjoyable leisure time activities for less enjoyable working time—in line with traditional economic reasoning. More relevant, however, is the person's global evaluative (cognitive) judgement of his/her life circumstances. Unemployment leads to a loss in self-worth because it causes a loss in social purpose, status and identity. An unemployed person may suffer from a permanent loss of identity, since he no longer belongs to the social group of workers and does not meet the respective social norm of 'being employed'. These psychological consequences of unemployment lower well-being much more than the pecuniary burden of unemployment. The fact that textbook models of labour supply neglect these aspects of working life beyond income and leisure yields wrong predictions about how to deal with the burden of involuntary unemployment. Even very generous unemployment benefit schemes cannot restore the subjective well-being lost when people lose their jobs.

Of course, one could argue that the difference in the reported subjective well-being may not be psychological at all, but merely represent the worsened future income prospects due to having become unemployed. This purely economic reasoning fails, however, to explain the empirical finding that life satisfaction of unemployed people increases substantially once they retire. Retirement does not change future income prospects anymore as the future income path is already determined right before retirement. Furthermore, unemployed people who retire also do not change their daily routines. Hence, the increase in life satisfaction must have to do with a change in the perception of one's own social status and social identity. When an unemployed person retires, he is still out of work, but no longer identifies himself with the social category of people of 'working age', but rather with that of people of 'retirement age'. Retirees do not have to adhere to the social norm of having to be employed anymore, which restores their sense of social identity and, thus, the well-being they lost when they became unemployed earlier.

# Saints in Public Office

## Gerhard Schwarz

>> *If only we had the right people in government, then everything would be fine. This is an illusory idea. We should focus on checks and balances and leave as much decision making power as possible to individual citizens.*

It might not be an entirely economic idea, but one that is very common among economists and policy wonks: If only we had the right people at the top of government, then everything would be alright and the economy would thrive. John Maynard Keynes expressed this idea in a letter to Friedrich August von Hayek in June 1944, reacting to Hayek's famous *The Road to Serfdom*, praising it as a "grand book," but then continuing: "... Moderate planning will be safe if those carrying it out are rightly orientated in their own minds and hearts to the moral issue...What we need is the restoration of right moral thinking—a return to proper moral values in our social philosophy...."

To ground economic policy in this way of thinking is fallacious on several accounts: First, everyone, independent of their position, is somehow self-interested; moreover, there is nothing wrong with that. Officeholders will regularly experience tensions between their personal and the general interest, regardless of their moral values. Second, there is no reason why public officials

G. Schwarz (✉)
Progress Foundation, Zürich, Switzerland

© Springer International Publishing AG 2017 **127**
B.S. Frey, D. Iselin (eds.), *Economic Ideas You Should Forget*,
DOI 10.1007/978-3-319-47458-8_54

should be morally better than people in other spheres of life. To quote Blaise Pascal's famous saying, they too are "ni anges, ni bêtes." They will sometimes put their interests first, they will not always behave morally, and, occasionally, they will violate their own and society's moral principles. Third, since moral values are not evenly distributed, but rather bell shaped, it is impossible to guarantee that only those with the highest moral standards will hold high public office. The idea that only the morally best will be in charge of the state and economic policy must remain wishful thinking. Fourth, power corrupts, and absolute power corrupts absolutely, as Lord Acton pointed out. Therefore, even those with the highest moral values might, once in office, change their thinking and their behavior for the worse.

Of course, we all know that "the right moral thinking" on one hand and the rule of law on the other are communicating vessels. A society with a high level of broadly distributed moral values can get along without a very elaborate and dense legal framework. Therefore, this is not an argument against morality, but an argument against the belief that we can select the morally best people for public office and thereby protect the freedom of citizens. We should not put our hope in public-minded people working wholly for the public good. Plato's philosopher kings would lead to a totalitarian state and a stagnating society.

On the contrary, in search of an open and free society, we should stick to the following guidelines: We should, as much as possible, align private and public interest for those in office, as we try to align the agents' interests with those of the principal within companies. It is entirely a question of incentives, be they monetary or otherwise. Further, we should create a legal framework, which gives those in office not too much leeway. Since we cannot rely on their moral standards, we have to make do with the same instruments that are applied in other realms of society whenever we want to avoid misuse of power—adopting rules and clearly sanctioning any violation of these rules. And lastly, we should leave as much decision power as possible to the individual citizen—and as little power as possible to the collective, the state, and those who hold public office.

# Helicopter Money

## Hans-Werner Sinn

> **»** *Forget about manna from heaven in form of helicopter money. It wrongly assumes that too little money is in circulation or that there is an inefficient starting position. The first claim is plain wrong and the second could already be tackled via traditional lending.*

Monetary policy has lost its effectiveness in the last crisis. For this reason, some economists argue that the central bank should increase its clout by distributing helicopter money, transferring money to all its citizens to be used at their own discretion. Unlike the loans normally issued by the central bank, this money would actually make people richer without harming anyone, they claim.

In their view, helicopter money is like manna from heaven. Citizens could buy more goods and the state would not be burdened. Even prominent economists have argued in favor of this idea.

However, issuing helicopter money is the same as the monetization of public debt. Whether the state posts a promissory note to its central bank and then distributes the new money to its citizens or whether the ECB distributes the money makes no difference with respect to the question of

H.-W. Sinn (✉)
Ifo Institute, Munich, Germany

© Springer International Publishing AG 2017
B.S. Frey, D. Iselin (eds.), *Economic Ideas You Should Forget*,
DOI 10.1007/978-3-319-47458-8_55

whether any gains would accrue to the citizens. And although the state must pay interest on its loans, these payments flow back to the state in the form of profit distribution by the central bank itself. In this respect, the manna argument, if it were correct, would also be a justification for the ECB's QE policy, which consists of purchasing government securities that previously went into circulation via the debt financing of budget deficits.

But the argument is wrong and should be quickly laid aside. It assumes that too little money is in circulation or that there is an inefficient starting position, in which a Pareto improvement is possible without rivalry for resources. Conversely, if the money supply is already appropriately sized, increasing this supply always means additional inflation that takes away the same amount of real wealth from existing money holders as the beneficiaries received in additional funds from this policy.

To be sure, the proponents of the manna theory may argue that precisely such an inefficient starting position is what we have today. But even if they were correct, it does not follow that helicopter money would have the manna advantage. The wealth effects of monetary expansion via the traditional means of the central bank lending fresh money to banks are in fact identical. With the creation of money from loans, the central bank and the state receive permanent, additional interest income flows, whose present value corresponds to the increasing money supply. If this interest income is used for transfers to citizens, exactly the same benefits are created as from helicopter money. The only difference would be that the government, a democratically elected body, decides who gets the resources rather than the ECB council, a technocartic body without a democratic mandate for fiscal policy measures.

# Decisions Are Deterministic

## Didier Sornette

**»** *The zombie idea that decisions are deterministic is still walking among us, although, both from an empirical and theoretical point of view, they have been shown to be inherently probabilistic.*

The *homo economicus* assumption that decision making is a deterministic process has been shown to lead to many paradoxes when confronted with real human decision makers. As a response, bounded rationality and a number of alternative theories have been advanced, such as cumulative prospect theory and configural weight models. In addition to failing to solve all fallacies and creating many novel ones themselves, these behavioral theories remain fully deterministic, while there is compelling empirical evidence that people do not make deterministic choices, i.e., they do not seem to settle on the choice that exhibits the largest desirability (whether this desirability is quantified by some expected utility or prospect value function).

Many studies have demonstrated preference reversal in situations when the same choices are presented to decision makers twice, with large frequencies (~30–50 %) of reversals for choices between alternatives for which decision makers are split almost evenly and still 10–20 % even in the presence of a clear majority. Such observed frequency of preference reversals derives and can be

D. Sornette (✉)
ETH Zurich, Zurich, Switzerland

quantitatively predicted without adjustable parameters, just on the basis of the observed fraction of decision makers making one choice in the first iteration of the experiment. Moreover, all existing models of decision making have limited in-sample and out-of-sample predictive power, saturating at a success rate level of 75–80 %. If decision making has indeed a coin toss-like component, one can never come up with a theory that will predict 100 % of decisions. There is an irreducible randomness. Taking into account this probabilistic choice component allows one to quantitatively evaluate the maximum predictive power, which turns out to be the observed empirical range. Thus, the natural interpretation of these effects is the intrinsic probabilistic nature of decision making.

In contrast, the standard approach is to combine deterministic theories with choice functions. For instance, cumulative prospect theory has been supplemented with the probit or logit functions. In one interpretation, these choice functions are technical devices added to the deterministic theory to allow for its calibration in experiments, with the implicit or explicit understanding that the stochastic component of the choice may result from the unknown component of the utility of a decision maker or hidden to an observer trying to rationalize the observed choices. Another school of thought considers choices as still being deterministic (the decision maker strives to choose the best alternative), but they make errors either in the evaluation of the alternatives or in the implementation of their choice. It is "as if" decision makers make nondeterministic choices, but in fact they are deterministic according to a hidden (to the observer) complex utility. The standard way of using such a stochastic approach is to assume a probability distribution over the values characterizing the errors made by the subjects. Stochastic decision theory and probabilistic choice theory embody the resulting stochastic element.

In contrast, decision field theory and quantum decision theory consider the choice process, including deliberations, hesitations, and subconscious estimation of competing outcomes as intrinsically random. The probabilistic decision is not just a stochastic decoration of a deterministic process, but is an unavoidable random part of any choice. Within an evolutionary framework, it is possible to show that being stochastic may actually augment the chances of survival and reproductive success in the changing, uncertain dangerous environments that characterized homo sapiens' evolution over most of the last 200,000 years. In that sense, probabilistic choice may be our innate adaptive characteristic rather than mere error deviating from deterministic decision making.

# Politicians Systematically Converge to the Median Voter

David Stadelmann

**》** *The median voter model is elegant. However, to understand actual political behavior it is not sufficient. Time for political economist to get their hands dirty by digging deeper.*

Studies in political economy, public choice, and political science frequently compare what politicians do with what their voters want. The textbook median voter framework serves as the central building block for numerous models of policy choice. Theories on the scale and scope of government, taxation, and redistribution regularly rely on the median voter model. It predicts that politicians converge to the preferences of the median voter due to the forces of spatial electoral competition and representation of the median voter is a stable equilibrium.

Despite its theoretical appeal, empirical evidence strongly points against the convergence implied by the median voter model. Findings from different sources show that legislative shirking is highly prevalent. If the median voter was decisive for policy choices, macroaggregates should correspond to the preferences of the median voter, which is not the case. Examining positions taken by politicians in the political space reveals that they diverge systematically from the median voter. Direct evidence for divergence comes from

D. Stadelmann (✉)
University of Bayreuth, Bayreuth, Germany

© Springer International Publishing AG 2017
B.S. Frey, D. Iselin (eds.), *Economic Ideas You Should Forget*,
DOI 10.1007/978-3-319-47458-8_57

**133**

confronting referendum decisions with parliamentary votes on identical issues. When individual politicians' actual policy decisions are compared to observed voter preferences in binding referenda, divergence from the median voter is the norm.

Numerous factors explain divergence and influence the behavior of politicians. They include candidate selection within parties, campaign contributions, difficulties in predicting constituent preferences, district characteristics and heterogeneity, entry of new opponents, incumbency advantages, individual characteristics of politicians, institutional constraints, interest group affiliations, multidimensionality of the policy space, partisan pressure and ideological purity, expected voter turnout, voter incomes, and winning margins, just to name a few. While these factors offer nonspatial explanations for failing convergence, they interact with each other, with the preferences of voters, and with the behavior of politicians: Candidates are selected by a party, making intraparty dynamics relevant, and selected candidates cannot credibly shift positions afterward, which leads to political alienation of the median voter and lower turnout. Thus, the fundamental workings of spatial electoral competition are affected by nonspatial factors. Theoretical research has mostly neglected to specify the conditions and institutional requirements under which the spatial explanation of the median voter model would or would not hold in the presence of diverse and competing incentives faced by politicians and voters.

The long-lasting appeal of the median voter model stems from its theoretical elegance, which makes it a great textbook case to focus ideas on electoral competition as one centripetal force. However, to understand actual political behavior and to predict policy choices reliably, the multitude of different incentives under changing institutions must be taken into account. Political economists will have to get their hands dirty to grasp politics more completely. Beautiful but overly simplistic theoretical models will not get the job done.

# Artists Are Poor and thus Unhappy

## Lasse Steiner

**»** *Artists do not fit into the standard economic model of labor supply, they work more, earn less, and are still happier than other workers. Time to focus on the process rather than the outcome.*

A popular view in economics, supported by numerous claims, is that artists are poor and unsuccessful and, thus, must be unhappy. Artists such as Franz Kafka, Emily Dickinson, Vincent van Gogh, Paul Gauguin, or Franz Schubert, all of whom were unsuccessful artists during their lifetime and, in some cases, mentally ill, have received considerable attention in the public, art history, and philosophy. The persistent popularity around the link between creativity and mental illness may just be notionally rooted in society's need to regard both genius and mental illness as "deviant." However, the artistic labor market is indeed marked by several adversities, such as low wages, above-average unemployment, and constrained underemployment. Artists earn less, on average, than they would with the same qualifications in other professions, and their earnings display greater inequality than those of their reference group. They suffer from above-average unemployment and constrained underemployment, such as non-voluntary part-time or intermittent work.

L. Steiner (✉)
CREMA – Center for Research in Economics, Management and the Arts, Zurich, Switzerland

© Springer International Publishing AG 2017    **135**
B.S. Frey, D. Iselin (eds.), *Economic Ideas You Should Forget*,
DOI 10.1007/978-3-319-47458-8_58

Nevertheless, the field of the Arts attracts many young people. The number of students by far exceeds the available jobs.

The classical economic explanation for this paradox is that artistic labor markets are superstar markets and artists are more risk loving. Another explanation from the realm of psychological economics states that artists overestimate the likelihood of future success. Both explanations are outcome oriented, focusing on the income artists derive as a *result of their work*. Jointly with coauthors, our research focused on a different approach, which emphasizes the importance of the process or the satisfaction artists experience *during their work*.

We found that artists are on average considerably more satisfied with their work than nonartists. The higher satisfaction is driven by superior "procedural" characteristics of artistic work, such as the variety of tasks, on-the-job learning, and opportunities to use a wide range of abilities and feel self-actualized at work. An idiosyncratic way of life, a strong sense of community, and a high level of personal autonomy, reflected by the higher self-employment rate among artists, contribute to the higher satisfaction. The relationship between income and job satisfaction is positive for artists and nonartists, as anticipated by classical economics. However, compared to nonartists the relationship is weaker for artists. This means that a higher income increases artists' happiness, but less so than the happiness of nonartists. Interestingly, the assumption of the neoclassical models that working more hours makes individuals unhappy does not apply for artists. Working longer hours does not decrease their job satisfaction. As artists do not fit the standard economic model of labor supply, it would be wise to dismiss the notion of the poor and unhappy artist. Considering the satisfaction people can and do derive during their work or other activities, not only focusing on the outcomes individuals obtain, has the potential to further progress in economic research.

# Returns on Educational Investments Are Highest for Early Childhood Interventions

## Elsbeth Stern

>> *The earlier the better, that's the economic mantra in educational investment. However, that is an oversimplification.*

Education economics has quickly risen as a research area over the last decades, with a major focus on the "return on investment" perspective. Quality of education obviously matters for societies' economic success and welfare—an insight that has stimulated the search for worthwhile educational investments ever since. In modern societies, education is mainly financed by the public sector, and it has turned out to be a bottomless pit. There are almost endless opportunities to invest the limited resources available. Just to mention a few examples: Should extra money go into gifted or special education? Should one buy computers for the students or hire additional teachers? Should teachers' salaries be raised in order to attract more competent applicants? These are all legitimate questions and in most cases there are pros and cons for each possibility, which does not make decisions any easier.

However, when it comes to the question, at what age level maximum payoff is achieved, economists' answer is straightforward: the earlier the better. This goes mainly back to the 2000 Nobel laureate James J. Heckman, who considers unfavorable child-rearing environments, predominantly in poor families,

E. Stern (✉)
ETH Zurich, Zurich, Switzerland

© Springer International Publishing AG 2017                    **137**
B.S. Frey, D. Iselin (eds.), *Economic Ideas You Should Forget*,
DOI 10.1007/978-3-319-47458-8_59

a major obstacle to a society's economic success. A lack of cognitive stimulation and emotional support in early childhood has negative effects on school performance and thereby prevents people from fully realizing their talents and contributing to economic success. Moreover, the burden on societies is even greater because those who failed at school run a greater risk of living on welfare or getting tangled up with the law. Investing in education is of general societal interest, and for Heckman it goes without question that the best payoff results from enriching children's environments before they even enter school. He came to this conclusion by comparing effects of early interventions with remedial education programs starting at school age or during vocational training. He seconds his arguments with results from neuroscience on rapid synaptic proliferation in early childhood. Like many others, he mistakenly seems to think that this indicates a more pronounced malleability of young children's brains. Sensible periods are assumed to exist over the entire scope of competencies, and windows of learning opportunities are feared to close if children do not get the adequate input at the appropriate time. In the meantime, it is well known that these concerns are exaggerated and based on inappropriate interpretation of findings from neuroscience.

Moreover, from a scientific point of view, Heckman can be blamed for overgeneralizing the unique situation of the USA, which is a wealthy country with millions of children nonetheless growing up in poverty, without healthcare, and in communities that fail to guarantee minimum standards of schooling. Most other developed countries also struggle with the problem of educational inequity, but not to the same extent, not even close. For many countries, it has been shown that high-quality elementary and secondary school education can compensate for unequal starts. Prioritizing investments in early education may be worthwhile for the special situation of the USA, but it should not be understood as universally applicable or based on generally valid scientific insights.

# EU Centralization

## Armin Steuernagel

**»** *Centralization in the EU leads to positive spillover effects and should be pursued. Wrong. The EU's highest potential lies in its diversity.*

Over the last decades, the European Union developed from the little-institutionalized European Coal and Steel Community to the much-institutionalized union we see today, with its own parliament and regulatory power in many areas. Although the public support of the transfer of more competencies to the EU has dwindled, officials and politicians see the solution to today's challenges in more power at EU level.

Two of the main arguments to justify this transfer of competencies and the increasing centralization are (1) its spillover effects and (2) its economies of scale. Especially the single market of the EU, so the first argument goes, needs policy coordination (e.g., in economic policy, labor market policy, or monetary policy) because of the—potentially negative—externalities. On the question of economies of scale, pooling the risks of different countries' bonds to a Eurobond may give every EU member a cheaper access to money.

It is important to take these arguments seriously but the usual answer, to centralize power, is problematic—especially in the EU. It does not address Europe's most defining characteristic: its diversity. Historically, the continent

A. Steuernagel (✉)
Department Political Science, Columbia University, New York, USA

© Springer International Publishing AG 2017                    **139**
B.S. Frey, D. Iselin (eds.), *Economic Ideas You Should Forget*,
DOI 10.1007/978-3-319-47458-8_60

is well known for the high diversity of its civilizations, cultures, and institutional arrangements, all within a relatively small region. Many claim that this is the reason for the European rise and success story. This diversity is at stake if we allow for strong centralization at the EU level. Even if the EU had strictly benevolent rulers in Brussels, it would still be impossible to have all necessary information to regulate this complex diversity centrally. It is even less possible to generate real democratic legitimation and debate, which leads to compromises taking all these differences into account. "One-size-fits-all" solutions are the natural result, making decentralized solutions impossible and leaving people feeling governed from the top.

I suggest the opposite. A new approach to centralization has been proposed by Bruno Frey and Reiner Eichenberger under the name of Functional, Overlapping, and Competing Jurisdictions (FOCJ). It proposes that individuals, communes, and regions have the right to build jurisdictions from the bottom up and form new authorities that have the power to tax members, work democratically, and are focused on a singular function (e.g., schooling or regulating rivers). On the one hand, they are overlapping, allowing parents, in the case of schooling, to be a member of either a French, German, or entirely new school jurisdiction independent of their location. On the other hand, borders can overlap and jurisdiction size can vary to suit the task. These entities will be competing because they allow for democratic participation— exit and voice. These flexible units can be instituted step by step, and many similar arrangements already exist—the Schengen area, for instance, which also includes non-EU countries. The project European Campus is another example of interest-specific grouping. Five universities on the upper Rhine have combined into a "free science zone" with the goal of overcoming national, administrative differences that would otherwise impede the exchange of ideas. Similarly, Swiss Cantons, German and Austrian Federal states, and Lichtenstein combined to form the "Bodenseekonferenz," tasked with environmental protection, the promotion of tourism, and other overlapping areas of mutual interest.

# The Alleged Asymmetry in Maintaining a Fixed Exchange Rate

## Jan-Egbert Sturm

**»** *Today's economic textbooks state that there is an asymmetry in the sustainability of a fixed exchange rate regime when facing appreciation or depreciation. This view is crumbling.*

To discuss the consequences of a given exchange rate regime, textbooks in international monetary economics or international finance generally simplify the different regimes down to two cases: a flexible vs. a fixed exchange rate regime, whereby for ease of interpretation, the world is often summarized by two countries and hence two currencies. Under a floating exchange rate regime, market participants active on the exchange rate market determine the value of the nominal exchange rate by acting on fundamental information and whatever else is driving their expectations. In the second case, at least one central bank has promised to trade the foreign currency for a specific amount of the home currency. As long as the economic fundamentals are in line with the declared exchange rate, making the central bank's commitment credible, supply and demand on the exchange rate market are likely to meet without the need for central bank intervention. However, when supply does not meet demand, the central bank will have to act on its promise. To alleviate upward

J.-E. Sturm (✉)
KOF Swiss Economic Institute, ETH Zurich, Zurich, Switzerland

© Springer International Publishing AG 2017

**141**

B.S. Frey, D. Iselin (eds.), *Economic Ideas You Should Forget*,
DOI 10.1007/978-3-319-47458-8_61

pressure on the home currency, it will buy foreign reserves, while depreciation pressure will be countered by selling foreign reserves.

In short, under a fixed exchange rate regime, the foreign reserves of a central bank adjust as demand and supply shift. A peg is sustainable if these shocks offset each other within a reasonable period of time. If these shocks, however, have a clear bias, then the peg turns out to be unsustainable. However, the likelihood of becoming unsustainable is considered to be extremely asymmetric. Whereas it is generally assumed that a central bank can accumulate foreign reserves indefinitely and thereby withstand appreciation pressures, once foreign reserves are depleted, or markets foresee a depletion, a central bank will have to give in. At the other extreme, buying up foreign reserves implies an increase in money supply which creates inflationary pressure. This leads to a loss in competitiveness and ultimately to a weakening of the country's economy and thereby currency. Therefore, it is often presumed that a central bank can indefinitely fight upward pressure its currency faces.

In early 2015, the Swiss National Bank (SNB) has shown that this is an apparent oversimplification. On January 15, it decided to no longer defend what was called the lower bound of the Swiss franc (CHF) against the euro (EUR), which was introduced at 1.20 CHF per EUR on September 6, 2011. The feared further increase in foreign reserves and the associated risks did lead the SNB to withdraw this policy. Whereby the structural trade surplus could be a fundamental factor underlying this pressure to appreciate, the strong deviation from purchasing power parity would be a counterargument when looking at the underlying fundamentals.

Instead, it was the fear that the about-to-be-introduced quantitative easing measures by the ECB would force the SNB to absorb large parts of those, combined with a gradual crumbling of the, albeit still strong, support of the lower boundary in Swiss politics and society, which formed the rationale for abandoning the lower bound. Only the mere fear of a further increase in foreign reserves itself, and thereby the balance sheet, is not sufficient to explain its dismissal. One strain of thought is that the implied increase in money supply could trigger higher inflation. In the case of an undervalued currency, this could and probably should materialize, but it would merely imply the necessary correction in competitiveness. If, on the other hand, the inflow is due to safe haven considerations and therefore would largely remain inactive in Switzerland, i.e. reflects an exogenous increase in the demand for CHF money holdings, hardly any inflationary pressure should result. In early 2015, there were no signs that inflation would breach Swiss policy targets in the near future, supporting the safe haven interpretation.

Therefore, if a lower bound can be expected to be maintained (indefinitely), no substantive increase in risks should occur. If, however, for whatever reason, the policy is no longer supported by society even a politically independent central bank like the SNB will have to relinquish its policy. The subsequent appreciation leads to a lower valuation of the existing foreign reserves and potentially creates substantial revaluation costs for society. Hence, combining both the expected increase in foreign reserves and the prospect of losing societal backing makes the lower bound policy risky. Solving such a model by backward induction makes a (one-sided) peg unsustainable today.

The difference in the sustainability of a fixed exchange rate regime when facing appreciation versus depreciation pressure does not appear to be as clear-cut as today's textbooks state. At the very least, we now have an interesting counterexample to trigger further research in the future.

# Governments Should Maximize the Happiness of the Population

### Alois Stutzer

---

**»** *It is a claim often made: Governments should maximize our happiness. But the claim is misguided for at least five reasons.*

---

The perspective of social welfare maximization in traditional economics is often perceived as a mandate of the state to maximize happiness. Modern happiness research, which develops informative empirical measures of subjective well-being, might be seen as an emerging science that has the capacity to finally facilitate the realization of this idea. I am convinced that it has great potential to contribute to the realization of happiness for individuals. However, a government decision rule, which aims at maximizing some empirical indicator of subjective well-being, is not the vision to pursue.

First, the idea of happiness maximization is based on the view that there is a benevolent and unconstrained government. Thus, the critiques of traditional welfare economics also apply to this approach.

Second, governments are assumed to agree on *the* happiness measure. The standards might, however, differ quite substantially across people: Some individuals might favor a reasoned ex ante evaluation, while others might wish to adopt a distant perspective reflecting on one's life ex post facto. Still others might emphasize the affective experiences of life as it is lived. Finally,

---

A. Stutzer (✉)

Faculty of Business and Economics, University of Basel, Basel, Switzerland

© Springer International Publishing AG 2017

B.S. Frey, D. Iselin (eds.), *Economic Ideas You Should Forget*,

DOI 10.1007/978-3-319-47458-8_62

there are individuals who sympathize with a cognitive appraisal of the overall quality of life as captured in evaluative measures such as satisfaction with life.

Third, a maximization of reported happiness reduces citizens to "metric stations." Rather than having a say on issues in politics, they become targets of mental state management. This disregards the fact that citizens have preferences for *processes* over and above outcomes. They gain procedural utility from living and acting under institutionalized processes, which offer them possibilities for self-determination in the economy and polity contributing to a positive sense of self.

Fourth, a mechanical implementation of happiness measures in the political process is likely to induce strategic interactions between government and individuals. Once a specific aggregate happiness indicator has become established as being politically relevant, the government, public bureaucracy, and various interest groups have an incentive to manipulate it. Similarly, when individuals become aware that the happiness level they report influences the behavior of political actors, they have an incentive to misrepresent it.

Fifth, empirical happiness research is not well equipped to make any normative judgments on the scope and limitations of government intervention in the private sphere. Should the government be allowed to prohibit the consumption of alcohol if it were to raise the population's happiness in the long run? Should those who adapt more easily to higher taxes be taxed at a higher rate? These questions cannot be answered on the basis of a happiness maximization calculus, but must be decided at a more fundamental level.

A theoretically consistent approach is to resort to the constitutional level, where people make such fundamental decisions behind the veil of uncertainty. Research and the idea of happiness for all have to serve the democratic idea of finding and agreeing on basic rules for all. The results gained from comparative institutional happiness research should be taken as inputs into the political process. These inputs have to prove themselves in an arena of political competition, in which citizens are free to openly discuss how the state should be organized so that people can best pursue their ideal of the good life.

# Okun's Equality-Efficiency Trade-Off

## Mark Thoma

**»** *Okun's equality-efficiency trade-off has become "law" for economists. In that sense, more efficiency comes with more inequality and vice versa. Forget about the "law's" characteristics.*

A little over four decades ago, Arthur Okun published *Equality and Efficiency: The Big Tradeoff*. In his book, Okun argued that redistribution to address inequality would suffer from the problem of a leaky bucket:

> The money must be carried from the rich to the poor in a leaky bucket. Some of it will simply disappear in transit, so the poor will not receive all the money that is taken from the rich.

The leaks are attributed to the administrative costs of taxation, the incentive effects on work for both those paying the taxes and those receiving the redistributed income, and from the resources used for tax avoidance. For many, this has become an economic law used to resist any attempt to address inequality.

However, there are many instances when both efficiency and equality can be improved. For example, a high degree of inequality can undermine support for

M. Thoma (✉)
University of Oregon, Eugene, OR, USA

© Springer International Publishing AG 2017
B.S. Frey, D. Iselin (eds.), *Economic Ideas You Should Forget*,
DOI 10.1007/978-3-319-47458-8_63

education and health programs for poorer members of society. Raising taxes on those with high incomes to build quality schools and provide affordable health care can increase economic growth. Support for social insurance more generally can lead to more entrepreneurship and increased labor mobility as people become more willing to move to take advantage of opportunities or take risks that can result in highly productive activities. On the other hand, there may be negative effects due to the higher taxes, though the incentive effects on the rich from higher levels of taxation are often overstated. In many cases these can be more than counterbalanced by the increase in productivity for disadvantaged members of society.

There are other examples as well. A high degree of inequality can undermine the social consensus that is needed to respond effectively to economic shocks, particularly in deep recessions when responses through both monetary policy and fiscal policy are needed. In a deep recession, where the costs of the recession fall disproportionately on those at the lower end of the income distribution while the costs of responding fall mainly on the politically and economically powerful, political opposition can stand in the way of the much needed countercyclical policy response. As recent research shows, longer, deeper recessions can have important long-term negative consequences for economic growth. A high degree of inequality can also create political instability, which is detrimental for investment and harmful to growth. In addition, as we saw on the 2016 campaign trail for the presidential nomination in the USA, high inequality can bring about a populist backlash that can undermine support for growth-enhancing activities, such as international trade. As a last example, when there is an excess of savings over investment resulting in secular stagnation, redistribution that takes advantage of differences in marginal propensities to consume can promote demand and make use of slack resources.

The relationship between inequality and efficiency is best thought of not as a "law" that holds for all levels of inequality, but rather as a Laffer curve-type relationship. Starting from a point of full equality, the positive effects of an increase in inequality outweigh the negative effects, and the net effect is an increase in efficiency. But at some point, the negative effects of increased inequality begin to dominate, and efficiency will fall. On that side of the equality-efficiency curve, an increase in equality can enhance efficiency and improve economic growth.

# "A Rising Tide Raises All Boats"

## David Throsby

>> *An overall lift in economic prosperity benefits everyone. Unfortunately, this is not true and economic growth is usually distributed unevenly.*

Although a nautical metaphor, it is much beloved by economists of a certain persuasion to argue that an overall lift in economic prosperity benefits everyone. John F. Kennedy used it often to justify various policy proposals. Kennedy was a president with many fine qualities, but expertise in economics was not one of them.

The rising tide proposition is frequently made in relation to economic growth—increases in GDP, so the argument runs, flow through to eventually improve the economic welfare of the population as a whole. It may be conceded that the payoff to some could turn out to be greater than to others or that it may take some time for it to be realized, but the universality of the improvement is seen as its justification. Indeed the metaphor must hold without exception if it is to be taken literally, since, when the real sea level rises, no boat misses out, and all boats rise by the same amount.

When it is applied to growth, there are at least two reasons why this picturesque and apparently irrefutable observation does not translate into economic reality. The first is that economic growth over any given period is

D. Throsby (✉)
Macquarie University, Sydney, NSW, Australia

© Springer International Publishing AG 2017
B.S. Frey, D. Iselin (eds.), *Economic Ideas You Should Forget*,
DOI 10.1007/978-3-319-47458-8_64

always uneven, with some sectors growing faster than others and some possibly declining. So a statistic showing an increase in aggregate GDP draws together a wide range of individual sectoral growth rates, some of which may be negative. The universality of the benefit is by no means guaranteed.

The second reason for the inapplicability of the metaphor to economic growth is a distributional one. Does it matter if, say, the top 10 % of the population enjoyed a 20 % increase in their income if the incomes of the bottom 10 % rise by only 2 % over the same period? "So what?" say proponents of the proposition, the poor are still better off than they were before. But of course there are equity concerns. The gap between rich and poor will have grown wider, other things being equal, and the negative consequences of increasing inequality in the distribution of income will presumably have been exacerbated.

A favored policy instrument to stimulate the economy and to increase prosperity is through cuts in the personal income tax. Rising tides are often eloquently referred to in this context, as Kennedy did. But this once again bears its share of problems. Many disadvantaged people don't pay income tax, if, for example, their income is below the threshold or they subsist only on welfare payments. So the tax cuts don't flow through to them at all. Their boat, if indeed they can be said to own one, is left stranded on the shore.

The usage of metaphor may serve a worthwhile purpose as a device for argumentation and communication in the social sciences. But the rising tide hypothesis is one that, as economists, we should forget. To mix metaphors, it simply does not hold water.

# Social Cost Analysis

## Robert D. Tollison

> **》**Social costs often get mixed up with private costs and are therefore counted twice, smoking being a prime example. It is time to stop the confusion.

Forget social cost analysis as it has been applied by economists associated with economic issues, such as obesity or smoking, the last of which be the basis of discussion here. The basic problem (as usual) is the confusion of social and private costs.

For example, the largest alleged social cost from smoking is the loss in production as a result of smoking. This argument is based on the larger absenteeism due to smoking and the earlier deaths of smokers, and these magnitudes are social costs largely borne by nonsmokers. The problem is that these are also private costs incurred by smokers. Lower productivity and higher absenteeism will be revealed in the wages of smokers as private costs, and to consider them as both social and private costs is double counting. Yet, every principles student dutifully learns this fundamental rule: Double counting is an error. To put it in another way, double counting leads to an underestimation of the benefits of smoking.

In remembrance of our great colleague Robert Tollison who left us in 2016.

R.D. Tollison (✉)
Clemson University, Clemson, SC, USA

© Springer International Publishing AG 2017
B.S. Frey, D. Iselin (eds.), *Economic Ideas You Should Forget*,
DOI 10.1007/978-3-319-47458-8_65

The second largest alleged source of the social cost of smoking is the cost of medical care for smoking-related illnesses. However, smokers may in fact die earlier and more quickly of, among other things, heart attacks, resulting in lower long-term medical expenses. Further, insurance companies typically offer reduced premiums for nonsmokers, the costs of which are covered by the insurance. This means that if the price reductions are counted once in the higher price of the smoker's insurance premiums, they shouldn't be counted again toward social costs. And lastly, there is no evidence that any medical costs are shifted to nonsmokers by the act of smoking. Again, this is an elementary error, which leads to an overestimation of the costs of smoking.

All of these fallacious arguments about the social cost of smoking have been propagated by "economists" and epidemiologists associated with medical schools, and they should be forgotten. They violate basic economic principles and bring no credit (except perhaps in the form of research grants) to their authors. These errors have also not stopped at smoking. We now have the economics of obesity, which makes the same basic double-counting error. If we continue at this rate, we will have "the social costs of everything," and it will be an open season on all behaviors that confused analysts find objectionable. "Mind your own business" is a good advice here; otherwise, we will move toward a world of meddlesome policies, with corrective taxes on behavior that political majorities do not favor, and favored behaviors are subsidized. Consider the field day that the fallacious social cost analysis is already having with obesity—the soft drink tax and the Big Mac and red meat tax following close afoot. Surely, it is not the last.

Of course, environmental tobacco smoke (ETS), where nonsmokers may have to breathe the smoke of others, can be a real problem for social cost analysis. However, ETS does not call for a ban on smoking. One could easily imagine market-based solutions based on environments, where smoking is allowed or not.

These misuses of economics are easily forgettable. They violate basic economic principles and bring no intellectual credit to their authors. Economics is about real problems and not the ones made up by analysts involving fundamental errors in reasoning.

# Natural Resources Make Rich

### Rick van der Ploeg

> **》** *It has to be repeated many times as it is still a popular idea: Natural resources do not make a country rich, unless these resources are managed carefully.*

Many countries have experienced windfalls though discoveries of oil, gas, gold, diamonds, copper, or other minerals. These can constitute 80–90 % of government or export revenues for many developing countries. Such foreign exchange windfalls offer a unique opportunity for resource-rich countries to improve the future of their citizens by speeding up their growth and development path. The obvious policy is to transform subsoil into aboveground wealth whether it is through human capital, health, infrastructure, or sovereign wealth. By investing in the domestic economy or saving foreign assets, consumption can be permanently increased even long after the flow of windfall revenues has ceased.

Developed countries with good access to international capital markets should finance their investments by borrowing, not by using the revenues from resource windfalls. They should therefore put their revenues into an independently managed sovereign wealth fund exactly as Norway has done. If oil and gas prices fall temporarily, the country will dip into its fund and thus

R. van der Ploeg (✉)
University of Oxford, Oxford, UK

© Springer International Publishing AG 2017                    **153**
B.S. Frey, D. Iselin (eds.), *Economic Ideas You Should Forget*,
DOI 10.1007/978-3-319-47458-8_66

suffer less of a drop in consumption. If the fall is permanent, the country has to cut back consumption.

Developing countries with little access to international capital markets suffer from capital scarcity and suboptimally low investment. For these countries, the natural resource windfall should be used to lower the cost of borrowing and to invest in the domestic economy instead in a sovereign wealth fund. Part of the windfall can also be used to boost consumption of current generations, which are likely to be poorer than future generations.

Alas, this advice is seldom taken, and countries, thus, suffer from the so-called natural resource curse or Dutch disease. By not smoothing consumption, countries experience sharp appreciations of the real exchange rate and a consequent decline of non-resource, traded sectors, such as manufacturing, and a boom in non-traded sectors, such as construction. Since engines of growth are typically located in traded sectors, a temporary resource shock induces temporary declines in growth rates and a permanent drop in the level of GDP. Even if the windfall is invested in the domestic economy, the economy may suffer from absorption constraints, thus highlighting the need for an invest-to-invest strategy.

The notorious volatility of commodity prices further amplifies the curse, especially in landlocked countries with badly functioning financial markets. The curse is also worse in countries that have weak institutions, competing ethnic factions, constraints on current account transactions, and unrestricted capital flows. The huge capital inflows following a resource discovery can wreak havoc on such countries. The curse is also aggravated by rent-seeking, self-interested politicians and outright corruption, especially, as the brightest people of such countries are sucked into rent seeking rather than productive entrepreneurship.

Substantial resource windfalls make governments lose sight of the value of money and become myopic. It is no surprise that policies such as excessive borrowing, using resource wealth as collateral when commodity prices are high, almost inevitably lead to sudden stops when countries unable to service their debt after commodity prices crash. Other mistaken policies are investments in useless prestige projects ("white elephants"), buildup of excessive welfare states, import substitution strategies based on import controls, and big subsidies for state industries.

These economic and political pitfalls of harnessing resource windfalls for growth and development are the reason that so many resource-rich countries experienced drops in non-resource rates of foreign direct investment, stagnating incomes per capita, and disappointing growth performances. The curse manifests itself also in terms of rising levels of inequality and poverty. There are countries such as Botswana, Malaysia, and Chile who have escaped the curse, but these are the exceptions to the rule. Sadly, natural resources do not necessarily make rich.

# The Natural Rate of Interest Is Positive

## Carl Christian von Weizsäcker

**》** *There might have been a time when the natural rate of interest was positive. But this time is long gone. As the roundaboutness of production has reached its productivity-maximizing level, today's natural rate of interest is negative.*

The natural rate of interest was defined by Wicksell as the real rate of interest on the capital market, which equates saving and investment under conditions of prosperity (full employment). Preceding Wicksell, Eugen von Böhm-Bawerk postulated three facts of life, which together induce a positive natural rate of interest. First, people want to shift their consumption of goods through time relative to the moment they accrue to them by earning (labor) income. However, while forward-shifting goods is possible by storing them, backward shifting is impossible. This gives goods that accrue earlier a higher value than goods accruing later in time. The second fact of life is "time preference," as Irving Fisher would call it later, while the third Böhm-Bawerkian fact of life is the positive marginal productivity of greater roundaboutness of production, which implies that firms prefer to use labor inputs earlier rather than later.

The modernized Böhm-Bawerk theory is consistent: based on the assumptions, a positive rate of interest is the natural conclusion. However, two

C.C. von Weizsäcker (✉)
Max Planck Institute for Research on Collective Goods, Bonn, Germany

© Springer International Publishing AG 2017
B.S. Frey, D. Iselin (eds.), *Economic Ideas You Should Forget*,
DOI 10.1007/978-3-319-47458-8_67

additional facts of life may invalidate these assumptions. First, storing goods is costly. Thus, an equilibrium may arise in which the present value of future goods is higher than the value of present goods. And second, there may exist limits to the greater productivity of greater roundaboutness of production. Beyond a certain threshold, further capital deepening may no longer provide any additional returns to labor productivity. The marginal productivity of capital may become zero or even negative. Thus, it is not a foregone conclusion that the natural rate of interest is positive.

While the capital-output ratio has remained largely unchanged, the world is a very different place 125 years after Böhm-Bawerk's "magnum opus." While the degree of roundaboutness may not have risen, it is much easier today to finance investment. Further, the first fact of life of Böhm-Bawerk (the propensity to shift consumption through time) now points strongly in the direction of a lower natural rate of interest. The massively increased life expectancy is one contributing factor: today, workers live another 20 years after retirement—in 1889, it was 2 years. This tenfold rise in the motivation to save for old age has led to an average savings-to-labor income ratio of 33 %. Bequests to children or other beneficiaries have also become substantially more important.

Due to the fact that the roundaboutness of production has reached its productivity-maximizing level, at a real rate of interest of zero, there is an excess supply of capital. Thus, the natural rate of interest is negative.

The world economy would be in a gigantic slump where it's not for massive government indebtedness. The supply of capital has thereby been reduced to a level that corresponds to the capital requirements in the production sector of the world economy under approximate full employment. One third of total private wealth in OECD countries and China is held in the form of government debt, which includes the debt owed by the social security systems to present and future pensioners in exchange for their past social security contributions.

# Europe's "Skill Shortage"

## Joachim Voth

> » *There is no such thing as a skill shortage. Forget about that. It's about wages that are too low.*

"Labor shortages" regularly grace policy papers, speeches, and memoranda. There are shortages, apparently, of skilled labor in German industry, of programmers all over Europe, and of health care workers and other medical specialists in many countries, etc. Members of the chattering classes nod their heads in agreement when the topic comes up over dinner. But a moment's reflection shows that it is a thoroughly misguided concept and nothing more than a sign of intellectual sloppiness: there is no such thing as a skill shortage.

A severe shortage of Mercedes S-class limousines has suddenly come to our attention. No? Haven't noticed it? Me neither. Why not? Because if there is more demand, they simply make more. That is, at the heart of the problem with skilled labor—it takes time to train people, and not everyone is suitable to be trained at all, hence, the idea that there may not be "enough" of a particular type of labor, that some industry or sector needs workers but cannot get them. But what does it really mean? It means that, given current wage rates, some firms, hospitals, or government offices would like to hire more people but simply cannot find suitable candidates.

J. Voth (✉)
University of Zurich, Zurich, Switzerland

© Springer International Publishing AG 2017                    **157**
B.S. Frey, D. Iselin (eds.), *Economic Ideas You Should Forget*,
DOI 10.1007/978-3-319-47458-8_68

The obvious question is why wages don't rise to the point of balancing supply and demand. And that is where the problem seems to lie—labor shortages overwhelmingly afflict the relatively low-paid but high-skilled professions—doctors in Spain, nurses in Germany, and IT professionals working for the government. They all make ends meet, but their pay can be fairly low. Public employers often act as monopsonists and like to put people on a particular rung on the scale, based on some metric combining seniority and years of education, and while the private sector offers much better wages, it cannot compete. Similarly, where unions constrain wage setting for subgroups, because they emphasize equality, some highly skilled and hard to replace subgroups end up underpaid. That is the real meaning of "labor shortage"— some people are getting a raw deal because the laws of demand and supply aren't working for them. It is like a shortage of S-class Mercedes at a price of 10,000 €—well, there would be.

So, what's the answer? Apparently, Stalin is alive and well—at least when it comes to battling "labor shortages." Since prices cannot adjust, we should manage quantities, as in the glorious days of central planning. Instead of targeting Y million tons of steel production a year, the idea should be to import X thousand programmers from India, bring Portuguese doctors to Spain (while Spanish doctors flock to Britain to escape ludicrous salaries), and shift nurses from Poland to Germany. All this of course means that wages could then be kept at the same low level that created the "skill shortage" in the first place. In this fashion, one form of market imperfection, typically created by intervention, regulation, and collective bargaining, is compensated by the next anti-market intervention. One has to believe in the superiority of central planning to think that the supply of skills in a modern economy can be fixed like this.

Next time when someone tells you about skill shortages in Europe, ask about wages. Ask why people with degrees in economics or law don't retrain to be IT specialists or why doctors from your own country flock elsewhere. Markets may not always work perfectly, but central planning of labor allocation is not the answer.

# Taxes Are Paid Because of Expected Punishment

## Hannelore Weck-Hannemann

» *People pay their taxes because they expect to be punished otherwise. This seems reasonable, but it's too simplistic. The probability of detection and the penalty tax rate do not seem to exert a significantly deterrent effect on income concealing.*

Taxes or levies have been around in some form or other for a long time—and, thus, so has been the problem that people have an incentive to avoid this tax burden. Tax authorities' efforts to collect taxes have, correspondingly, always been present and, given the temptation to cheat, also been quite pronounced. In democracies, tax revenues allow for the provision of public goods, and, thus in turn, governments are interested in avoiding tax evasion.

The standard approach to analyze tax evasion relies on one of the central tenets of economic theory: the relative price effect. If the price of a commodity rises or it is more expensive to carry out a particular activity, it is expected that this good or activity is less attractive and less demanded accordingly.

The traditional economic theory of tax evasion does not question this negative relationship: a risk-averse individual chooses either the amount or the share of income to be concealed so as to maximize their expected utility of income, while considering the probability of detection, the penalty tax rate

H. Weck-Hannemann (✉)
University of Innsbruck, Innsbruck, Austria

© Springer International Publishing AG 2017
B.S. Frey, D. Iselin (eds.), *Economic Ideas You Should Forget*,
DOI 10.1007/978-3-319-47458-8_69

applied if tax evasion is detected, the marginal tax rate, and the level of true income. Accordingly, theoretical studies based on this standard economic approach and the relative price effect conclude that both the probability of detection and the penalty tax rate will negatively affect underreporting of income.

The economic policy conclusion is straightforward: higher penalty tax rates and more control, along with a higher probability of detection of illegal behavior, should help to combat fraud, and, as a result, tax revenue should rise.

However, empirical findings do not confirm this relationship: the probability of detection and the penalty tax rate do not seem to exert a significant effect in deterring income concealing. Though the coefficients of the measures of control and punishment may have the expected negative signs, they are generally not statistically significant.

This lack of significance does not comply with the traditional model of tax evasion, but rather with an extended version that includes the interaction of citizens and the government. The standard portfolio selection model of tax evasion fails to specify how tax revenues are used by the government. Tax evasion is analyzed as a "game against nature," considering neither how government revenues are raised nor how revenues are spent.

The extent of citizens' (dis)satisfaction with the supply of public goods and, consequently, their (un)willingness to contribute toward the financing of government have to be examined. This can be done, e.g., by focusing on the different institutional arrangements of collective decision-making in alternative democracies. Studies of such alternate institutional arrangement largely confirm the qualitative hypotheses of such an extended model: the extent of political participation of citizens/taxpayers has a clear and stable effect, thus indicating the substantial influence of policy acceptance on taxpayers' adherence of tax laws.

This result suggests an extension of the standard economic approach to tax evasion with respect to institutions. Only when the interaction between citizens and government is fully accounted for and the often cited aspects of (tax) morale are endogenized can the model provide a proper base for tax compliance policies. It becomes evident that the existing incentives to noncompliance cannot simply be removed by refining the public control and penalty system and thereby increasing the number of decisions made for rather than by the citizen/taxpayer. Both aspects, taxes and public revenues, as well as the interaction between citizens and the state, must be taken seriously and under consideration.

# Better Safe than Sorry

## Antoinette Weibel

**>>** *Better safe than sorry sounds like good advice, but it's not. People with a high disposition to trust and therefore with a less safety-orientated attitude are less likely be betrayed.*

Following Williamson's core assumptions, we ought to "(a) [...] not contract in a naïve way" and "(b) mitigate opportunism cost-effectively". However, looking at current figures, his credo has certainly failed when it comes to cost-effectiveness. Studies suggest that transaction costs amount to 50–60 % of any developed country's GDP. Some scholars claim that "bullshit jobs", which consist of mainly controlling, monitoring, and sanctioning behaviors to prevent opportunism, are even on the rise. Standard economists are likely to argue that these figures come from temporal inefficiencies, which will be resolved in the long run! But is that really the case? I argue that the assumption of opportunism effectively prevents cost-effectiveness!

First, assuming opportunism to prevent hazards hampers learning from failures. For instance, trust research provides clear evidence that human beings with a high disposition to trust, i.e. who approach relationships with an open and non-suspicious mind, are less likely to be betrayed than those with a distrusting mindset. Why? Because individuals with a trusting stance learn

A. Weibel (⊠)
University of St. Gallen, St. Gallen, Switzerland

© Springer International Publishing AG 2017
B.S. Frey, D. Iselin (eds.), *Economic Ideas You Should Forget*,
DOI 10.1007/978-3-319-47458-8_70

more about human nature and, as a result, develop high emotional intelligence—a compass to "smell the traitors". Also, starting transactions with a leap of faith often evokes reciprocity and hence impedes others from acting upon their self-interested instincts. In addition, available experimental and field evidence demonstrates that leaders can even "fall" into a vicious learning cycle, the so-called "paradox of surveillance": leaders who assume that their employees are prone to self-interest exhibit strong surveillance behaviors. However, by monitoring their employees (too) closely they miss the opportunity to learn whether their employees, given a chance, would honor their trust or not. Due to this lost opportunity, information asymmetries between leader and employee tend to remain higher than necessary.

Second, as argued by Ghoshal and Moran in their famous article, a distrusting stance leads to opportunism instead of preventing it. By now, we have ample evidence that distrusting, autonomy-thwarting monitoring crowds out intrinsic motivation for both the job and trustworthy behavior and will thus lead to opportunistic behavior. We also know from previous research that expecting others to fail to meet our expectations begets distrust. Numerous articles show how such vicious distrust cycles evolve. Furthermore, distrust has been linked to different areas of the brain and a different hormonal system than trust. Hence, once distrust is evoked, no room is left for trust. Finally, relatively new evidence from neuroeconomics suggests that performance management based on distrust and enacted in ranking and grading systems provokes "fight-or-flight" responses of those ranked. These systems ultimately undermine performance rather than fueling it. Summing up, in a more dynamic view, "better safe than sorry" leads to much more "sorry" than warranted.

Are we thus only left with naïve trust as an alternative? Not necessarily, controls can support trust—what matters are the intentions of the controller. Controls that signal good intentions and trust toward employees enable positive reciprocity and drive intrinsic motivation precisely because they are not based on the premise "better safe than sorry".

# The End of Work

Boris Zürcher

>> *One idea that should be forgotten is that we will soon run out of work, and it therefore needs to be better distributed in order to prevent large-scale unemployment.*

Strictly speaking, the idea of the end of work is not part of conventional economics. However, even great and eminent economists are not immune to its charms. A prominent example is John Maynard Keynes, who in his 1930 article "Economic Possibilities for our Grandchildren" succumbed to it. He speculated that, within a century or so, productivity would attain such high levels that *the economic problem* will be solved. In Keynes own words:

> I draw the conclusion that, assuming no important wars and no important increase in population, *the economic problem* may be solved, or be at least within sight of solution, within a hundred years. This means that the economic problem is not—if we look into the future—the permanent problem of the human race.

In the same article, Keynes also coined the expression of *technological unemployment*. "This means unemployment due to our discovery of means of economizing the use of labor outrunning the pace at which we can find new

B. Zürcher (✉)
State Secretariat for Economic Affairs SECO, Bern, Switzerland

© Springer International Publishing AG 2017
B.S. Frey, D. Iselin (eds.), *Economic Ideas You Should Forget*,
DOI 10.1007/978-3-319-47458-8_71

**163**

uses for labor." Maybe intended as a slight provocation toward his contemporaries, he concluded that "3-hour shifts or a 15-hour week" would be enough to accomplish "what work there is still to be done."

The idea that we will soon run out of work because of technological progress and because of an ever-increasing productive capacity has inspired many more, not only economists, but philosophers, intellectuals, and, in particular, politicians, who pretend to apply simple common sense and basic arithmetic reasoning. Politicians tend to blame economists for being excessively optimistic and naïve, when as the politicians maintain, the facts are certain and a clear-eyed view of the world as it really is shows that work definitely will disappear.

Surprisingly, advocates of the idea of introducing work-sharing programs, parceling out work, and reductions of the workweek are not inspired by the current record high unemployment rates across Europe. Instead, they tend to be influenced by the fear of digitalization and the spread of robots, which they think will depress labor demand and ultimately make human labor altogether superfluous. Add to this globalization and global division of labor that are exacerbating the problem.

Yet, we, as economists, also fail to praise the achievements of a more productive economy. We lack answers to questions like what to do with the ever-increasing supply of goods. Conventional wisdom associates technological progress and expanding productivity with more production only.

And finally, where are new jobs going to be created and will income continue to grow? Our failure of imagination is the root of the problem we need to address in order to visualize tomorrow's labor market. With the advent of digitalization, for example, job profiles, which 25 years ago would have meant nothing to the majority of people, have become the norm. History shows that every structural change, every "revolution" has brought forward intense changes in the labor market. They have created new jobs, new opportunities, and new possibilities for gainful employment.

However, it won't be science or politics leading the way or highlighting the opportunities. Economics lacks imagination when faced with the future of work. Human beings become either obsolete or despondent because "new" work is never seen as satisfying or challenging.

Yet, looking back in time, after more intense structural change than what we currently witness, new jobs, new opportunities, and new gainful employment emerged, and we have all gotten richer. This time isn't going to be any different. However, imagination is too much to ask from our dismal science.

# Postscript

## Bruno S. Frey and David Iselin

Economics is a rigorous and proud discipline ready to leave the past behind and to give up its formerly cherished ideas, concepts, and methods if they are considered to be false or no longer relevant. This even applies to the apparent foundations of economics. The collection of texts in this volume bears witness to this state of upheaval in economics.

In editing, we are very aware that the contributions in this volume do not present a representative view of economists. There are certainly scholars who would object to some, perhaps even most, of its suggestions. An economist reared in the traditional way of "doing economics" might very well be shocked by some of the propositions put forth by the contributors. Nevertheless, even a more or less representative sample of scholars will frequently find itself proclaiming ideas that are not in line with the profession's orthodoxy as it is presented in major textbooks. We have on purpose selected authors who we expect to have fresh and unusual views about economic science.

We want to push forward economics, following Schumpeter's dictum on "creative destruction". The views brought forward here constitute an excellent basis to further develop our discipline. The collection contains a great number of novel ideas worth pursuing.

B.S. Frey
Crema—Center for Research in Economics, Management and the Arts, Zurich, Switzerland

D. Iselin (✉)
KOF Swiss Economic Institute, ETH Zurich, Zurich, Switzerland

© Springer International Publishing AG 2017
B.S. Frey, D. Iselin (eds.), *Economic Ideas You Should Forget*,
DOI 10.1007/978-3-319-47458-8_72

Max Planck, the inventor of quantum theory, once said (or at least is believed to have said) that science advances one funeral at a time. He was talking about deceased scientists, not deceased ideas, but you have to let go of both of them.

John Maynard Keynes remarked in 1936s *General Theory of Employment, Interest and Money*: "The difficulty lies, not in the new ideas, but in escaping from the old ones, which ramify, for those brought up as most of us have been".

We hope that this collection of essays makes a small contribution towards overcoming this difficulty.

Druck

Canon Deutschland Business Services GmbH
Ferdinand-Jühlke-Str. 7
99095 Erfurt